Lost to the Sea

For Bryan Longbone

Lost to the Sea

Britain's Vanished Coastal Communities:
Norfolk and Suffolk

Stephen Wade

PEN & SWORD
HISTORY

First published in Great Britain in 2017 by
Pen & Sword History
an imprint of
Pen & Sword Books Ltd
47 Church Street
Barnsley
South Yorkshire
S70 2AS

ISBN 978 1 47389 347 4

A CIP catalogue record for this book is available from the British
Library

Typeset in Ehrhardt by
Mac Style Ltd, Bridlington, East Yorkshire

Printed and bound in Malta by Gutenberg Press Ltd.

Pen & Sword Books Ltd incorporates the imprints of Pen & Sword
Archaeology, Atlas, Aviation, Battleground, Discovery, Family History,
History, Maritime, Military, Naval, Politics, Railways, Select, Transport,
True Crime, Fiction, Frontline Books, Leo Cooper, Praetorian Press,
Seaforth Publishing and Wharncliffe.

For a complete list of Pen & Sword titles please contact
PEN & SWORD BOOKS LIMITED
47 Church Street, Barnsley, South Yorkshire, S70 2AS, England
E-mail: enquiries@pen-and-sword.co.uk
Website: www.pen-and-sword.co.uk

Contents

Chapter 1

Introduction and My Own Quest

The tide goes out for miles and returns at a canter. It is desolate. The wind whispers ... No men but naturalists disturb the solitude of the salt marshes.
H.V. Morton, *In Search of England*

The fascination of lost communities

A ll lost towns and villages fascinate us; even a single farmhouse quivering on a cliff, awaiting its doom, is compelling. There are many reasons for this: a story is about to end; livelihoods are in the balance; time has rubbed out something once thought to be permanent. All these are valid and interesting, but more than anything else, it is the thought of a community beneath the waves, an Atlantis, that really appeals to the imagination. As I write this, the British Museum is presenting a major exhibition called Sunken Cities, which concentrates on ancient Egypt and its connections with the classical world of Greece. Christina Riggs, appraising the exhibition, wrote, referring to Frank Goddio, a diver and archaeologist:

What Goddio's team has found are the port city of Thonis-Heracleion ... and Canopus, renowned in antiquity for the worship of Isis and Serapis. Both were submerged over a short period of time, probably by the end of the eighth century AD. In addition to long-term subsidence along the coast, core samples in the bay suggest that its sediment layers turned to liquid at some point, perhaps due to flooding or seismic activity. The cities collapsed under their own weight.

This explains the appeal: beneath the sea lie these former cities, now visited by divers and explorers as well as by sharks and shoals of fish. Their existence now is that of a barnacled toy place, deserted but still largely intact. It could be an image from a dream resplendent with thoughts of Jules Verne's Captain Nemo and his *Nautilus*, or from the undersea world of Jacques Cousteau. It is a place we cannot easily walk into.

But the lost places off England's coast are not so romantic, and my subject being a tranche of the east coast, the following events are likely to be recalled with a shiver. The sense of an Arctic wind will stream through my words, not the tranquil azure surface of the Mediterranean. After all, lost places are tombs of a kind.

There is something of a personal quest in this book too. I first went to East Anglia in 2002, to teach a weekend course at Belstead, near Ipswich. I could see a good slice of Suffolk in the vista from the garden but I had no time to explore what I could see. Then, a little later, I spent a week in Gorleston, among boats and seashore, but instead of confronting the sea and the cliffs I went inland and saw Bury St Edmunds, Snape and Diss. I lingered in Walsingham, as one is supposed to do. When was I going to see the sea? This was a sea that had been an inspiration to poets, writers and landscape painters for centuries. I had read about it and fancied I knew it instinctively, as if I had dreamed of it. This was intensified by my affection for the Fenland books of Edward Storey, which I had read avidly for years. For this work, I had to put together the notion of the fens with those of the coast; I saw that in writing their history, their inter-relationships must be absorbed.

Then, at last, I went for a week in North Norfolk, and among many visits to the shore and the cliffs, one stands out today. I took a long walk northwards from Old Hunstanton towards Brancaster, and there the beauty hit me like a revelation of what the first sunlight must have been. That is, I experienced the sheer magnitude of the vision the Norfolk coast can give. Yes, there was that menace of thinking exactly what may be eaten up by sand and gale-force winds, by angry seas and hungry tides. But before all that was this breathtaking splendour of nature, with the kind of light that generates spiritual awakening: a light above and between that special admixture of sea and cloud that the big sky of East Anglian can give.

I had to go back, and I had to write about the place. I knew that. It's been a long time coming, but this book is two things in one: it is at once the story of a lost Norfolk and Suffolk, and also my own record of the discovery of a slice of England that captivates people and draws them to know what *wonder* is. That sense of wonder is needed now more than ever, as the utilitarian world encroaches on what poets have called, ever since the days of ancient Rome, the *numinous* view of the world – the sense that there is something divine behind some places. It could be called spiritual if one wanted to steer away from religion, but whatever draws one to these sea shores and the magnificence of the North Sea, it is a force that goes on inspiring and energising.

Nevertheless, I wrote the stories of these lost communities because, more than anything else, they represent something quintessentially East Anglian. There is a vast library of sources and narratives concerning this coast, from the marshes of The Wash by King's Lynn down to Dunwich and Southwold. The main reason for this is the affection so many writers and painters have had for this part of England. Norfolk and Suffolk have had their chroniclers, and most of these writers have opened up the nature of these counties to a massive readership. Notable amongst them are three men – Ronald Blythe, Ronald Fletcher and Rowland Parker – who have shown the great march of history by means of the micro-history of one little place. Their books – *Akenfield*, *In a Country Churchyard* and *Men of Dunwich* respectively – have done much to reveal those qualities of the life and people of these two counties through a successful mix of poetry and documentary, all imprinted with the unique narrative voices of the writers.

I felt their presence hanging over me as soon as I planned this book. Would I be able to imbue at least a modicum of that poetry into my social history? Well, I have certainly tried.

Writing about places that are no longer there seems at times to be as fruitless as Don Quixote's deluded activity of tilting at windmills. But there is a difference: human habitations that are now no more than fragments on a sea bed or a shingle bank have back stories. These dwellings were once lived in; as markedly as any other vestige of a once-known life, they have records. The records may not be shelves of cardboard files in archives, but they are there to be discovered if one looks in the right places.

Along the coast from Brancaster down to Aldborough, their names are, or have been, on the maps through the ages. These images may be informative but they are also chillingly fearsome. They show what was once the 'German

Ocean', now the North Sea – a great expanse of threatening water, the marine equivalent of the Killing Fields. On Thomas Milne's map of the Norfolk coast of 1794, the words over the shaded areas off the coast have a daunting resonance. Happisburgh Sand and Happisburgh Gatt are marked, beyond the brief notes alongside the place names: 'Cliff 50 feet high', 'Mud cliffs from 20 to 30 feet high' and 'Eccles in ruins'. By the village of Palling we have 'beaches filled up'. At times, it is difficult to comprehend that contrast between the fragility of the mud cliffs and the happy holiday venues of 1930s railway posters.

The Dunwich Project

In the summer of 1932, a memorial service was held on a Suffolk cliff. It was for a once great and impressive cathedral city called Dunwich, which had had a bishopric as early as 630. The sea had made considerable progress in drowning the place as early as the mid-eleventh century. In the middle of a meadow, a tent was placed, so that Father Davison could say mass. Later in the day, a procession of pilgrims went to the crumbling churchyard on the edge of the cliff, to gather and perform a blessing to the sea. When this was done, everyone returned to the tent and the celebrity guest, the famous Father Ronald Knox, preached a sermon.

Dunwich, of all the settlements lost to the sea, has received perhaps most attention, and it is easy to see why. It had been a busy port. At one time the place had a population of 3,000 and had three churches; the last of these tumbled into the sea in 1919. In the 1200s, there had been friaries and a thriving market. In fact, monks of all major orders had settled there. The fact that the memory of Dunwich was marked with such ritual is completely understandable.

Seven years after that last church was lost, there was much attention paid to the villages named by Rudyard Kipling 'ports of stranded pride', and Dunwich attracted the attention of commentators from all quarters. One reporter described it at the time as 'the most tragic place on all the east coast'. This lost collection of homes and places of worship, of trade and sea-based trades, is between Aldborough and Southwold and has received more than its fair share of historical reappraisal. One writer explained that in the years of Edward I's reign, it maintained, 'besides eleven ships of war, sixteen fair ships, twenty barks or trading vessels to the North Sea and Iceland etc., and twenty-four small boats for the home fishery'. There had been a presentiment of things to come in 1286, on New Year's Day, when there was flooding, and in the following year, much worse inundation followed.

There had never been a problem on the landward side. The Earl of Leicester had once tried to lay siege to the town in Tudor times, and a chronicle notes that 'the strength thereof was terror and fear for him to behold'. But as with Ravenser and many other coastal towns, the troubles of the hungry waves began to intensify in the fourteenth century. In 1328, not only was the harbour utterly demolished, but 400 homes went, victims to the water. Then, in 1740, hills of almost 50 feet in height were flattened by the floods, and such was the devastation that graves were flushed out and skeletons came out, lying in the water, as one writer put it, 'scattered as the surges carried them'. That is undoubtedly a horrific image. No corpse is free from removal in the face of such force. In 2007, as the water level of the stream in Grasmere rose alarmingly, there were fears that William Wordsworth and relatives would become visible skeletons. In Dunwich in 1740, the sight was an unmistakeable sign that something needed to be done. But could anything be done in the face of such a foe?

In 1926, a press reporter described the situation, with the last church in mind:

> When last your correspondent was here the considerable Church of All Saints still stood a landmark from far out to sea, derelict but practically complete, with a narrow footpath along which it was possible to pass between its eastern buttresses and the cliff's edge. Today there is only a little hummock of masonry, grass-grown, marking where the footpath ran.

Dunwich has presented something far more resonant, with fear of time's erasure of humanity, than geographer and broadcaster Nick Crane's sight of the footprints in the stone: the cliffs have yielded scraps of the long narrative of death and dissolution that has marked Dunwich as a community condemned to be as permanent as the shifting sands of Arabia.

One man's memory will illustrate this. In the 1920s, he wrote, after inspecting the soft cliff:

> Presently, one of our party saw, some 4 feet below him, a little row of white points just protruding from the perpendicular wall. They were dreadfully like human teeth. Almost at a touch from a walking-stick above them, a miniature avalanche of the hill above them fell away, and there was a skull, upright, as if its owner stood upright, staring with deep, sightless eyes straight out to sea. By dropping to a lower shelf, it was easy to reach it and so it was lifted, with the severed lower jaw replaced, laid gently on the turf where it was hoped the Coastguard or someone in authority would give it safer burial *again*.

The last remaining grave at Dunwich was of Jacob Foster, and some bones such as those found in the above example were placed by his grave.

Some may have called Dunwich 'England's Atlantis', but marine archaeology is arguably a stronger force applied to the location than folklore or myth. The *Fortean Times* online community has enjoyed long discussion of the supposed undersea bells heard, from anywhere on the Norfolk or Suffolk Coast, but more solid information has come from dives and other studies. For instance, new searches have revealed various wrecks, such as one at the northern end of the harbour, and another that has been dated after c. 1750. The report notes that 'the wreck is wooden with copper sheathing on the hull' and the vessel is 30 metres long. Along with these details comes more information on the town itself, such as proof that roadways and ditches were definitely of Saxon origin, and that there is evidence of a Saxon rope-making industry.

The Dunwich Project goes on, as science goes to work on the lost community. Even the television *Time Team* enterprise has been at work, in 2012, and one report notes that the Maison Dieu (the name used for the Hospital of the Holy Trinity) was located under a café at present on the beach. Obviously, plenty of underwater pictures have been taken, and analysis continues.

There is no doubt that the landmark of All Saints Church is an excellent signifier of the sea's destruction over the centuries. Drawings of that building from 1736 to 1930 show a change from the full, very long church and tower through to the first major break-up of the rear section of the building in 1903, and then the accelerated ruination up to 1930, when all that was left to see was the almost completely wrecked tower standing in the water.

Dunwich is perhaps the most prominent location along the massive stretch of undersea terrain going from Northern Scotland down to the Channel that has been called Doggerland. The Department of Earth Sciences at St Andrews University has been at work on this and the staff have produced an exhibition on the 'Drowned Landscape' of this area. Richard Bates, of the university, told the press:

> Around 20,000 years ago there was a 'maximum' [wave movement] although part of the area would have been covered with ice. … Through a lot of new data from oil and gas companies, we're able to give form to the landscape, and make sense of the mammoths found out there, and the reindeer. We're able to understand the types of people that were there.

The exhibition tries to imagine the Mesolithic populations of Doggerland, and it has taken combined work from St Andrews, Birmingham, Dundee and Wales Trinity St David universities to create this. Sketches show the probable human settlement – wigwams, pits and fires – along streams. What have been found are the probable locations at which settlements occurred.

All this suggests 'Atlantis' as a label for the imagined mass lying under the North Sea; to try to create a concept of a string of lost villages along this shelf is to invite the folklore as much as the findings of scientific inquiry. But Dunwich stands out as special in many ways, largely because of work done by the historian Rowland Parker, who set to work on resurrecting the nature of Dunwich and its people in his book *Men of Dunwich*, in 1978.

Parker also wrote the modern classic of micro-history, *The Common Stream* (1975), and he had an exceptional ability in bringing out the materiality of medieval times, mixing documentary and social history with a real feel for life as lived. Parker went to school in Louth, at the Grammar School (where Tennyson also was once a pupil), and then became a teacher of French before enlisting in the Royal Artillery in 1940. He lived in an old cottage after the war, in Foxton, and while there spent over a decade researching for *The Common Stream*.

Parker's love of hands-on history is shown in his archaeological work too: he was in the excavation team at a Roman villa in Shepreth, in south Cambridgeshire; among the significant finds was a carnelian gemstone. Then came the book on Dunwich, a place he loved. Parker died in 1989. His account of Dunwich makes it clear that the town's troubles accelerated in the first thirty years of the fourteenth century. The storms and tides of 1328 have been referred to, but to build on the importance of that period for the loss of the place, reference may be made to a work by Thomas Gardner, published in 1754. He took material from records of the bailiffs, where it is noted that in 1334 there were only a few houses left in three parishes that were at the edge of land. So extreme were the weather and tidal depredations, Parker explains, that the people took all kinds of materials out of the church of St Leonards, thus saving them from loss. After 1328, there was a mass emigration from the town. There is no doubt that the third decade of that century saw the first major phase of the eradication of Dunwich: it made the sands of King's Holme move southwards and the harbour was actually covered and shut off.

Rocks and people, stories

Norfolk is predominantly standing on clay. This may only be seen in the fens, apart from at the sea cliffs. The great clay ridge beneath the grass can be observed very clearly at the coastal side at the cliffs in Hunstanton. There is an upper layer of rock simply labelled 'upper chalk' and then the massive layering of chalk marl beneath. In the remains of forests found down in the rock, Pliocene life is evident. As early as 1900, writers on this were imagining the areas to the west of what was to be Doggerland. For instance, W.A Dutt, in 1902, wrote:

> Mr W.F. Harmer suggests that during this period the Rhine swung round in a great bend from Kessingland to Cromer, following more or less the present trend of the coast. The bones of many large animals have been discovered in the forest bed, including those of two species of elephant, hyena, musk ox, whales etc.

This is a feature of virtually all the east coast, as, for instance, at Sutton in Lincolnshire, where historian Nikolaus Pevsner, looking at local churches in 1960, commented: 'Along the road at low tide stumps of trees can be seen belonging to a submerged forest about 4,500 years old.'

When Dutt wrote those words, he was working at the very time that some of the Norfolk villages were close to the end of their existence, and he noted, in writing of Eccles-by-the-Sea:

> The parish is reduced now to only a few acres by sea encroachment. The round tower of its church, around which the sand-dunes were at one time so high-heaped that it was possible to walk into the belfry windows, fell in November, 1895.

This little former fishing village sets the pattern for many lost Norfolk communities. At the time of the Domesday Book there was a settlement with 2,000 acres. It survived reasonably well over the centuries until the flood of 1604 (mentioned earlier) had a major impact. We know this because the inhabitants wanted to pay less tax, as there was then much less land. The record shows that all that was left of Eccles by then were fourteen houses and 300 acres of land.

At the close of the nineteenth century, it was reduced to a couple of farms and only seventeen people. Today the remaining land consists mostly of the Bush Estate, a collection of bungalows. The decisive modern formative event, as for most of the east coast, was the great flood of 1953. This finished off some remnants of the place.

Obviously, as was the case with Dutt's comment on Eccles, it is always the loss of the church in a village that takes prominence, and in the case of Eccles, the church in question was St Mary's. Its story acts as a template for the stories of lost churches along the coast through the centuries. The storms of 1570 did considerable damage. Then, centuries later, the sand dunes were clogging more stone, and by 1893, the chancel ruins were evident on the beach. Largely because of the efforts of a local photographer, it is possible to see what the building was like: it had a round west tower and an aisle to the south. The church had lasted since the twelfth century.

The undersea bells?

Maybe there are the sounds of bells from beneath the waves off Norfolk and Suffolk – who can be certain? Many people have reported the supposed phenomenon off Cromer where the village of Shipden was lost. Of this coast generally, a good idea of what has gone may be gleaned from the maps made by the great cartographer John Speed in 1610. Many communities have been swamped and drawn away, including the grandly named Eccles juxta Mare, but Shipden has attracted more reference.

From the Cromer pier, a view out to the north, to a point at about half a mile, lies Shipden. The 1086 Domesday Book reported a population there of over a hundred inhabitants, as well as the usual meadows, trees and domestic animals. Along with the old adage that 'as sure as God's in Norfolk …' there were churches there, catering also for the hamlets of Felbrigg and Crowmere. In the reign of Henry III, William de Wayland owned much of Shipden, and after him it passed into the hands of the famous Paston family. Other land at Shipden was held at this same period by Roger de Reymes.

One note in the records gives us some idea of the wealth of some Shipden people: a parson of the village called Robert Brown, along with Roger de Hederset of Billingford, paid by fine to Clement Hervey of Shipden, 'fourteen messuages [a house with outbuildings and orchard], a mill, two lofts, 150 acres of land, 4 of meadow, and 2 of pasture, 2 of wood, 46 of heath and 36s in rent'. In 1422, a certain John Gees owned most of the village.

After the sea and centuries did their work, Shipden, along with every other Norfolk place, looked to its economic resources and to holidaymakers. Of course, it was part of Cromer in a practical, trade-centred sense. Throughout the nineteenth century, the struggle went on, and as Shipden went under and life in Cromer itself went on, there were dangers caused by the submerged village. On 9 August 1888, a vessel struck Church Rock, which marks the site of Shipden. *The Morning Post* gave all the facts:

Early yesterday morning … a steam tug, carrying about 200 excursionists from Cromer to Yarmouth, ran upon a rock near the former place yesterday afternoon. The vessel soon began to show signs of sinking, and passengers quickly became aware of their dangerous position. They were greatly alarmed, but fortunately perfect order was preserved. There were only two boats on board, but the position of the steamer had been quickly noticed from the shore, and help was soon sent. All the passengers were landed without mishap and subsequently reached Yarmouth by train.

It was not the only casualty on that fateful day: the fog that night claimed many more victims, including five excursion steamers, which all stuck fast in the mud on the river Tamar.

Shipden, as it is so close to Cromer, has given rise to the more fanciful imaginings of visitors and locals with a taste for the paranormal. It might be going a little too far, however, to suggest that Arthur Conan Doyle, staying in Cromer in 1901, where he conceived the notion of writing *The Hound of the Baskervilles*, perhaps heard of the dangers of the sea frets and perils of the shifting sands. Certainly, though, the idea of a town below the sea and the rising fog that endangers shipping would seem to run parallel to Grimpen Mire in the writer's imagination. Other literary men knew the effects of the Norfolk floods from the sea with a more practical eye than any folklorist. H. Rider Haggard, for instance, owned land at the coast, and he wrote in his book, *A Farmer's Year*, in 1899, referring to the previous year:

> Never has such a time for high tides been known, and the gale of December last will be long remembered on the east coast for its terrible amount of damage. The site close to a house which I possess at Kessingland, a place near Lowestoft, was something to remember, for here and at Pakefield the high cliff has been taken away by the thousand tons. In such a tide the fierce scour from the north licks the sand cliff and hollows it out till the clay stratum above it falls. ... Fortunately for me my house is protected by a sea wall and though the water got behind the end of this, it did no further damage.

Cromer, by the 1870s, had everything needed to inspire confidence in the visitor. One handbook from that time makes it clear that the old forest survivals from ancient times would be an attraction, and indeed that is still the case today, as the tree remains are seen on the beach by the pier end. The handbook for Victorians quotes the great geologist Sir Charles Lyell:

The forest bed consists of the stumps of numerous trees, standing erect, with their roots attached to them, and penetrating in all directions into the loam of ancient vegetable soil on which they grew. They mark the site of a great forest. … It is exposed in certain seasons and states of the beach.

There is much more to the East Anglian coast than the physical geography expressed in terms of facts and statistics, of course. A walk along the marshes and shingles of any stretch of coast between Brancaster and Cley, for instance, will give you the pleasures of the terrain and the wildlife, but also, as astronomer Mark Thompson has reminded us, plenty to see looking upwards. He writes:

Norfolk skies are among the best in the country for sky watching. Not only are they dark because of a lack of light pollution, but the rural nature of the country means industry is all but absent and the resulting pollution is not clogging up the sky.

It is a joy to experience the great open vista this coast gives you, and ironically, it is the cliff erosion that adds to this aesthetic pleasure, as the disintegrating rock and soil has its own beauty.

I shall return to Cromer and Shipden later, because their story is like that of a twin who has lost her partner, and lives with an empty space where the love should be.

Chapter 2

From Doggerland to the Normans

Spits and forelands are the coast's oldest appendages, impermanent ethereal places with unique human narratives.

Nick Crane, *Coast*

The elusive past

How do communities start? What is the process by which they emerge from land, from certain locations? In the case of the Norfolk coast, writer and historian Hilaire Belloc was given an explanation by a local at King's Lynn back in the early 1920s:

The town would begin upon the highest of the bank, for it was flatter for building, drier and easier to defend than that part next to the water. Down from the town to the shore the fishermen would lay out their nets to dry. How nets look when they are so laid, their narrowness and the curve they take, everybody knows. Then on the spaces between the nets shanties would be built, or old boats would be turned upside down for shelter, so that the curing of fish and the boiling of tar could be done under cover. Then as the number of people grew, the squatters' land got value, and houses were raised … but the lines of the net remained in the alley-ways between the houses.

It all makes sense, and seems to be so simple. But of course, the history of land settlement in Britain offers a wide variety of different development patterns. One of the most meticulous of social historians, Peter Laslett, has pointed out a feature of Norfolk that while not disagreeing with Belloc's interviewee, stresses the paradoxical notion that there has always been isolation in spite of widespread settlement:

Norfolk has no less than 660 ancient parishes, and in that most prosperous of the shires in earlier times, there were 969 medieval churches; you can sometimes see ten aspires or towers from one vantage point. Yet even in Norfolk, on the Breckland, there are miles and miles of desolate landscape where few dwelt and where the settlements are well out of sight of each other.

So the counties of East Anglia have always been rather hard to reach. Even today, there are no motorways across from the A1 in Norfolk. But what about the very early times? We need to start with some account of this land when the people existing there were hunter-gatherers, and the point when that began to change and some little communities began to build something to gather under, even if that was merely a shelter of animal skins over a network of tree branches.

On a coast such as this, hundreds of years ago, everything would start with the harvest of the sea and what was needed by the people who wanted food and a place to settle. The old man at King's Lynn was thinking, of course, about a recognisably modern community, but what about the very ancient times, before settled communities? The story of the Norfolk and Suffolk coast begins with some account of our knowledge of the prehistoric phases of land formation along the east coast.

At this point there is a need to explain some geological terms. As far as my purpose here is concerned – looking at the human communities on this coast over time – what matters is a period known to geology as the *Quaternary Era*, a two-million-year expanse of time within which the human race was the life form of most prominence. Inside that broad term Quaternary are the terms *Pleistocene*, in which there was an ice age, and the *Holocene*, the time scale since the ice receded, about 10,000 years ago. At our point in history, we exist in an interglacial period. As geologist Richard Fortey explains, Norfolk and Suffolk are the perfect locations in which to study the processes and materials associated with 'construction and destruction, between sediment and erosion, between ice and warmth'.

This period – the Quaternary, and within that, the Holocene – are, in geological terms, very recent. This means that the rocks are unconsolidated: there is no real elevation and the surface is composed of those sand-filled, encrusted rocks we think of in typical sediments by water. In East Anglia, these rocks are known as the Crags. Of course, this is all vulnerable to weathering, and there is yet another factor, according to research by scientists looking at the North Sea Basin as a whole and how Britain fits into that picture: Britain is on an angle, east to west, but there are some higher areas, such as the Cromer Ridge.

The work of archaeologist Clement Reid revealed a submerged area out in the North Sea. Reid was the great-nephew of Michael Faraday; his particular passion in science was geology rather than electricity. In 1913, Reid published a book called *Submerged Forests*, in which he suggested that there was an undersea land bridge that once joined Britain to Europe. He attempted a map, which prompted the beginnings of geological research into what is now firmly established as the place called Doggerland. Reid had joined the large-scale Geological Survey in 1874 and won several awards for his work.

In the Geology Society's obituary for him in 1916, we have this:

in 1876 he was transferred to Norfolk, and there began ... the detailed study of the Pliocene and Pleistocene deposits, including the 'forest bed' and 'contorted drifts' of the Norfolk coast. The name of Clement Reid has ever since been intimately associated with the study of these formations, and indeed, in all matters relating to the forest bed, he was regarded as the chief authority.

Reid's key work in this respect was *The Geology of the Country around Cromer* (1882). What he began has since been a major preoccupation of geologists, and Doggerland is now a place being explored by marine archaeologists from many countries. The Pleistocene age covers a period from about two million years BC to 10,000 years before the present; in that period there were glacial and inter-glacial ages, so with melting and freezing, the level of land would change. In the first phase of the Pleistocene, stages known as Cromerian, Anglian and Hoxnian were the periods in which much of the geological landscape and materials of the East Anglian coast were formed. For instance, Reid's work on the forest bed formation shows that at the end of the Lower Pleistocene, these beds had silts, gravels, sand and freshwater peat.

Geologists divide glacial ice sheets into 'older' and 'newer' in the geological timescale, but the whole area of land covering most of Yorkshire and Lincolnshire, together with all East Anglia, except the coastal fringe around The Wash, is classified as 'newer glacial ice sheets'. So, in terms of the massive scale of time on the geological charts, the coast of Norfolk and Suffolk is 'new', and that essentially means, unformed, in flux, friable and subject to erosion.

After the retreat of the ice about 10,000 years ago, lakes were left in the land and the sea coast changed radically. It is possible to envisage one continuous land mass stretching from the far end of Europe across to Britain, where clans of hunter-gatherers would have roamed, on the move until a time came when, alongside lakes or large estuarial waters, as in Norfolk, some kind of settlement began.

Doggerland lies there

We are quite accustomed to hearing the word 'Dogger' referring to one of the thirty-one sea areas of the British shipping forecast, but we perhaps have only the vaguest idea where that area is. A glance, the forecast chart shows it as a block just above another in the forecast designated 'Humber'. Doggerland has now become more specifically a name for a vanished mass of land from pre-history. The location of the undersea land in question is north from the Humber, but back in that post-glacial period before sea levels rose, the people from the north and the east would have moved across and then south to East Anglia, just as happened in North America. There was then a land bridge across what is now the Bering Straits, so that various peoples moved and settled from Alaska all the way down eventually to South America.

Doggerland (or as some call it, 'Northsealand') is really the first lost community in my history. It was a massive area of land beginning about 100 miles off Spurn and extending a long way north. Most recent thinking, emanating from the work done at Imperial College London and research by Gareth Collins and his colleagues, suggests that its end came when there was a 'tsunami' and subsea landslide off Storegga in Norway. These sources argue that it was abandoned about 8,000 years ago. The press have insisted on calling Doggerland the 'British Atlantis', and as work has progressed, more and more is being discovered about its people. A report by Paul Rincon for BBC News summarises what it was like:

> By around 20,000 years ago, the area would still have been one of the richest areas for hunting, fishing and fowling in Europe. A large freshwater basin occupied Doggerland, fed by the river Thames from the west and by the Rhine from the east. Its lagoons, marshes and mudflats would have been a haven for wildlife.

Rincon quoted Bernhard Weniger from the University of Cologne: 'In Mesolithic times, this was paradise.' But later, Doggerland was a low-level landscape, and estimates put it as about the size of Wales. The most exciting – and relevant – new research on Doggerland has turned up evidence of the humans who lived and worked there. Remains and artefacts have been found and traces of the drowned landscapes are gradually being revealed. The largest evidence is in the 'drowned forests' – groups of tree stumps that occasionally become visible. It seems that this terrain was one of deciduous woods, rivers and mudflats. A feature in a 2016 issue of *Current Archaeology* journal gives insight into what was there:

> At Tygbrind Vig, off the coast of Denmark, such stunning discoveries as textile fragments, wooden paddles, well-preserved Mesolithic dwellings – some with intact wall stakes – have all been recorded on the sea floor, preserved ironically by the waterlogged conditions that led to these communities being abandoned.

The feature also attempts to describe the intangible: 'Northsealand would have represented not just a home but a storehouse of memories and ideas: place is evocative, closely tied to memory.' This is exactly what the story of the Yorkshire Coast communities has to define, despite it being so fragmentary.

The undersea land had been imagined previously. H.G. Wells, a visionary in his fiction in so many ways, wrote a tale called *A Story of the Stone Age* in 1897. It is about a time when 'one might walk dryshod from France to England, and when a broad and sluggish Thames flowed through its marshes to meet its father Rhine, flowing through a wide and level country that is under water these latter days.' In the early twentieth century, Clement Reid began a search for the remains of Neolithic humans, and he wrote *The Antiquity of Man* in 1913. One of the highlights in the saga of this search for Doggerland was when, in 1931, a ship called the *Colinda* brought out of the sea off Norfolk a great peat clod, within which was a harpoon dating back to several thousand years BC.

It was Bryony Coles who gave Doggerland its name. She was the first to try to map the hypothetical position of the area. The evidence is now multiplying; geophysical modelling is being undertaken, and apart from the usual flint tools and such, the occasional find of a more startling nature is located, such as a huge fossilised mammoth bone. One researcher told the media, 'We haven't found an "x marks the spot" or "Joe created this", but we have found many artefacts and submerged features that are very difficult to explain by natural causes, such as mounds surrounded by ditches and fossilised tree stumps on the sea floor.' Much has been done by academics from the University of St Andrews, and the experts are gathering: climatologists, archaeologists and geophysicists. Dr Richard Bates from the university told the *Daily Mail*: 'Through a lot of new data from oil and gas companies, we're able to give form to the landscape – and make sense of the mammoths found out here, and the reindeer. We're able to understand the types of people who were there.'

The traditional view is that the cliff coast that submerged in very early times formed part of Doggerland. After the last ice age, about 6,000 years ago, the temperature rose and so did the sea level. Ice sheets had held the land down, and as the water melted, the land rose, much as we see in peat when it absorbs water compared with when it dries. The low-level settlements were submerged, becoming the first communities to be lost to the sea. This cannot have been sudden; settlers along the Doggerland bridge must have tried to combat the encroachment of the sea, just as their descendants were to do through the years that followed. Doggerland appears to have finally been lost under water about 7,000 years ago, and little sign of its existence remains.

There is also the further consideration of the sea bed and the coast itself: the nature of sand, and how that may be the instrument of smothering and eradicating homes and villages. The Doggerland settlements may well come into this category, and if we wish to see an example nearer to our own time, then the archaeology done at Kenfig on the coast of South Wales is available. The *Time Team* crew did some work there. Sand is just as destructive as wind or water. There was a settlement in the Bronze Age at Kenfig, and by the thirteenth century the sand was beginning to cover everything man-made. Eventually, the church there was relocated to Pyle. What is left at Kenfig, where there once was a castle, is an area of deep sand dunes. When *Time Team* arrived and set to work in 2012, they soon discovered how heavy and awkward a sandy dig was compared to soil.

After that last glacial retreat, concluding a succession of movements of glaciers and then the end of Doggerland as the sea level rose, we have to look to archaeology to have any idea about human settlement in the Early Bronze Age. Fortunately, there is the very impressive work done by the Norfolk Archaeological Unit, and their report prepared for English Heritage in 2005. This gives the lay reader the bare facts:

> The earliest evidence for human populations in Norfolk dates to about half a million years BP. Flint tools and *debitage* [materials produced by *lithic reduction* – the disintegration of rock into fragments] possibly from this date onwards, and possibly made by people of the species Homo erectus, have been found in several sites within the county.

The main basis for our knowledge is from Bronze Age barrow cemeteries, such as the one at Salthouse, and also the cemetery near Hunstanton. Fortunately, the report points out that there have been significant early human settlement finds:

> During the Iron Age a fort with massive earthworks was built at Holkham, close to the coast.... Three smaller defended enclosures are known close to the coast, all in North-West Norfolk. A hoard of 180 torcs [metal neck rings] was buried at Snettisham in about 70 BC and hoards of Late Iron Age continental gold coins have been found at Snettisham and Weybourne.

Early Settlements

Other information on these Bronze Age settlements has gradually come along, such as through the *Time Team* work at Flag Fen to the east of Peterborough. This is in a depression, with a dry landscape on all sides. Tim Taylor, writing about the *Time Team* work, explains: 'The picture that results is possibly unique in Britain and it shows a succession of landscapes and settlements, complete with burials and ceremonial monuments, that starts around 1300 BC and extends well into the Roman period.' The place has been reconstructed, and images show a roundhouse, turf-covered, in an enclosure of hurdles. There would have had to have been a high level of woodworking skills to make such a building.

Regarding the Roman period, there has been plenty of material found and sites have been studied and assessed in detail. Unlike, for instance, on the Yorkshire Coast, where the only Roman remains were of small signal stations, in East Anglia there was much more going on in the context of the Roman invasion following the arrival of Claudius's army in AD 43. Before that, in Caesar's time, there had been the failed attempt to land and conquer in 55 BC. They had arrived in a land of myth and legend, a fearful place, but they knew about its resources and treasures. Venerable Bede, in his *Ecclesiastical History of the English People* (c. AD 731), describes what the Romans found in these words: a 'boundless ocean' and a 'rich variety of many metals'.

In English literature, the Roman remains found in Norfolk have surely their most famous investigator in the person of Sir Thomas Browne, author of the classic *Religio Medici* (published 1643). He also wrote a strange work called *Hydriotaphia* or *Urn Burial*, in which he turns his enquiring mind to the urns left in Roman sites. This was back in the mid-seventeenth century, when amateur antiquaries were sifting through remains from all historical periods, asking questions about them from a limited scientific basis of knowledge. Browne gives one of the first accounts of this attitude to the past, hunting for answers about the Roman settlement around the area:

> That these were the urns of Romans from the common custom and place where they were found, is no obscure conjecture, not far from a Roman garrison and but 5 miles from Brancaster, set down by ancient

record under the name of Brannodunum. And where the adjoining town, containing seven parishes, in no very different sound … still retains the name of Burnham, which being an early station, it is not improbable the neighbouring parts were filled with habitations.

Famously, East Anglia's most prominent place in the story of Roman Britain was regarding the rebellion of the Iceni, led by Boudicca, joining forces with the neighbouring Trinovantes. But by the end of the second and during the third centuries AD, some kind of settled Romano–British culture was in place in East Anglia, and a series of coastal forts was built, probably around AD 200–230. The *Classis Britannica*, the Roman fleet, had gradually been reinforced and stabilised along all the east coast. In his survey of Roman Britain, Malcolm Todd has written: 'A reorganisation of the units disposed on the coasts brought new forts to Brancaster and Reculver.' He also explains that Caister-on-Sea was always an important fortification, and when he was writing, almost forty years ago, details were hazy:

> If Brancaster, Caister-on-Sea and Reculver all belonged to the same scheme of fortifications it is tempting to look for at least one other site on the coasts of Essex and Suffolk. Unfortunately, coastal erosion has been so severe that the Roman coastline has been engulfed by the sea, and with it, several Roman sites; a small town at Dunwich and a later fort at Walton Castle have entirely disappeared.

Fortunately, marine archaeology has helped to locate and describe the Roman sites. The report referred to earlier in this chapter points out that through the Roman and early Middle Ages period, significant geomorphology occurred – changes in land formations: 'Cemeteries have been found at Burgh Castle and at Caister-on-Sea and on the cliff top at Mundesley. That at Burgh Castle continued into the Middle Saxon period where a church and/or a monastery may have been built.'

Malcolm Todd raises the question as to why the Roman forts were built in the first place. His answer is that there was more of a threat to Rome in the early third century. He looks at reasons for attacks on this coast and concludes:

In the northern coastlands marine transgression was beginning to deprive some of the inhabitants of their lower-lying ground, but this does seem to have been so drastic as to compel them to seek homes far from their earlier dwellings. For the time being, moreover, there was land enough to accommodate a growing population. Attacks on the Roman provinces were therefore almost certainly piratical rather than indicative of land-hunger.

This is important because clearly, throughout the centuries in which Roman rule created a new culture, what is today East Anglia was well populated and that settlement included the coasts. Where the Romans built forts there would be clusters of a supporting ancillary community, just as, where Romans built towns, there was a *vicus*, a related settlement of non-combatants.

Of course, the next phase of development and settlement brought further influences, with the arrival of the Scandinavians. One of the key features of this influence, after the fights subsided, was summarised over a century ago by the writer W.A. Dutt, whose point here helps us to see the continuity and the settlement pattern that was established when William I had completed his Domesday Book in 1086:

> at the time when the Conqueror's survey was made, most of the occupiers of land were small independent freeholders. Of the 10,097 freemen mentioned, 4,277 were in Norfolk, 5,344 in Suffolk, 314 in Essex and only 162 in the rest of England, whereas in other counties colonized by the Saxons there is a preponderance of *servi* and *villani*.

The reference here is to a *villein* (*villani*, plural, in the Latin version), which was a word used to refer to a tenant on a manor who was unfree but had a share in the communal produce and the working of the system. *Servi* were the serfs, working on, and tied to, the land.

William I reserved ninety-five of the manors in Norfolk, and gave Roger Bigod ninety-five. Bigod's name is therefore bound to keep appearing in the various local histories here. For the present purposes, the material in the great survey is invaluable even if all settlement in a place is covered by a few farms and some barns and homes scattered around a few acres. At least that is some kind of beginning, something to compare with later statistics.

The *Victoria County History* of 1906 gives the reader a map showing the places mentioned in Domesday, and one of my most staggering revelations in researching this book has been the contrasts then and now. I am not the first to see this informative material. In *Suffolk Sea Borders*, published in 1926, seaman and writer H. Alker Tripp looked at the earliest records and then moved into a rhetorical voice to show his emotional response to the lost places:

> Where is Wadgate Haven, where the quays by Walton Castle, where is Dunwich? They harboured the ships of the Middle Ages, but the sea has overwhelmed them. They are drowned and gone. Where are the havens of Thorpe, Sizewell, Minsmere and Easton? The sea has retired and left them stranded.

Chapter 3

North Norfolk and The Wash

Some enchantment lies upon the coast of North Norfolk which leaves it in memory, not just an impression of peculiar beauty, but a series of pictures ...
Lilias Rider Haggard, *A Norfolk Notebook*

A place of isolation

The enchantment referred to above by Lilias Rider Haggard is partly one of slow change and isolation; her beloved Norfolk was always a place that was sparsely populated and resisted change. Even today, although thousands flock to the coastal resorts, there is no motorway helping them speed across the heath and pasture, and reaching the country B roads and tracks is sometimes challenging. But historians have often noted the slow changes. Barbara Tuchman, the great chronicler of the fourteenth century, for instance, commented in her survey of England around 1370:

> In the poll tax of 1379 four villages of Gloucestershire were recorded as making no returns; in Norfolk six centuries later, five small churches within a day's visit of each other still stood in deserted silence on the sites of the villages abandoned in the fourteenth century.

But after those six centuries, huge world events finally encroached on the peace.

In June 1944, Britain had good reason to be thinking about beaches and shores: the Allied invasion of Normandy was in process, and the press had pictures of German prisoners on the beaches awaiting transportation across the Channel to prison camps. It seemed the right time to the editors of *The Observer* to draw their readers' attention to the state of Britain's coasts. In a feature headed 'Britain can fight for her beaches – Seaside slums must go', there was a report referring to the work of 'Mr Steers, the Cambridge geographer' who had drawn attention to the parlous state of the coastline. Steers listed industrial development, 'ugly and misplaced huts and shacks, military and defence works and unregulated camping and caravanning' as the main sources of problems. *The Observer* reported: 'Miles of Lincolnshire and Norfolk coasts are disfigured by long lines of jerry-built wooden erections.'

Mr Steers concluded: 'The nation should take care of its coastline. We have only one coast and it is neither a local nor a regional, but a national possession.... Nothing less than a national policy will do.' Most people along the Suffolk shore are still waiting for that.

This had been the cry from experts as well as from businessmen and those who relied on the sea and on holidaymakers for their survival; but there had been no national policy, and the history of coastline protection and conservation at that time was one of ad hoc measures and action taken only by vested interests. For centuries there had been attempts to explain the problems and also to suggest remedies for such matters as erosion, sand deposition and flooding. Norfolk and Suffolk had been locations of special interest to those amateur writers and antiquarians who had given time to the problems.

It is a place of watery incursions, marshes and silt, as described by Graham Swift in his 1983 novel *Waterland*: 'What silt began, man continued. Land reclamation. Drainage. But you do not reclaim a land overnight.... The Fens are still being reclaimed even to this day. Strictly speaking they are never reclaimed, only being reclaimed.'

A scan of a modern-day detailed map covering the stretch of coast from Shepherd's Port around to Stiffkey shows a land with a vocabulary created by tough experience and relentless domination by weather and water. To the west, it starts with Peter Black Sand and then Stubborn Sand as far as Hunstanton; then the thick belt of sand continues past the old walking track of Peddar's Way by Gore Point; after that, Brancaster Bay opens out and Brancaster harbour leads to the dunes and shingle of Scolt Head Island and Burnham Overy Staithe, leading to the broad sweep of Holkham Bay and the dunes and salt marshes of Cabbage Creek and Stiffkey Freshes and Blakeney Harbour.

Beyond that, away from The Wash and along the coast towards Yarmouth, the string of villages and hamlets open to the sea's destruction continues. But the land on The Wash itself and the Fens to the south, was once, thousands of years ago, part of a massive ice-bound lake called Lake Fenland; there is a shrinkage going on. Geologist John Whittow has written: 'At Holme Fen, near Peterborough, some 4 metres of peat have been lost since the cast-iron Holme Post was buried in the fen in 1848.' So, it is not only coastal land that has been lost; it is also inland peat beds.

Travellers' tales

At the end of the seventeenth century, the intrepid woman traveller Celia Fiennes arrived in north Norfolk. Her experience is summed up by Nicholas Crane in his book on English travellers:

> Getting out of Norfolk was almost as difficult as getting in. West of Norwich the route to the Midlands was blocked by over 1,000 square miles of impassable fenland.... Her first sight of the Fens came as she made a barely perceptible descent from Chippenham House to the River Snail: 'I passed over a low ground on each side ... defended by the fen-dykes which are deep ditches and drains.... The Fens are full of water and mud.'

In 1671, forty years before the horrendous storm of 1703 that did widespread and savage damage to many parts of the land, an anonymous writer produced *A True and Perfect Relation of the Great Damages done by the late Great Tempest and Overflowing of the Tide*. At that time in the history of printing, short, snappy titles were not considered to be important, but the author's long-winded account of destruction was surely ratcheted up by the wordiness:

> Upon the coasts there are reported near twenty ships to be cast ashore and split, and most of the men drowned, although the Boston ships are all safe, but one; but yet the tide hath made the breaches in the banks. Upon the coast of Norfolk they speak of thirteen sail of Lynn ships that are known to be lost, and more feared. The tide came in so violently

that it hath born down the houses by the Far-Wash; the banks are all broken down from the Broads to Boston.

Twenty years before that there had been an ordinance made to try to revive an Act of Parliament 'for the recovery and preservation of many thousand acres of ground in Norfolk and Suffolk surrounded by the rage of the sea'. This had been ordered by Oliver Cromwell, a man from Huntingdonshire who would have known something about floods and the destructive powers of water.

In 1703 came the cataclysm. One famous witness to this horrific destruction was Daniel Defoe, who was later to write about Norfolk and Suffolk as part of his great tour of Great Britain, published in the 1720s. Nicholas Crane, in his book on travellers across the land, explains:

Published in 1704, *The Storm* was Defoe's eyewitness account ... of what is still billed as the worst storm in British history. An extra tropical cyclone, it smashed into Britain on 26 November 1703. Over 8,000 people perished. ... Defoe was there. He saw it. The destruction was awesome. He writes of ships thrown into tangled heaps on the Thames; of windmills catching fire because their cogs were spinning too fast; of houses and churches dashed to pieces ... there were countless shipwrecks. ... Once again, East Anglia had been in the front line.

Much of the Norfolk fishing fleet was lost in the week-long tempest.

In 1789, while most of the world worried about events in France, a certain M.J. Armstrong, a geographer and surveyor, was concerned about the coast of Norfolk. He had a lot to say about the value of marram grass in retaining soil. In Norwich, he read a paper to the Society for the Participation of Useful Knowledge, and this became a tract in circulation. Armstrong's paper is a valuable source of information on the coast at that time. Some of his statements explain the reasons why the coast here has been so ravaged by natural forces: 'The north-east coast, by Sheringham and Cromer to Happisburgh, is lofty, though torn and varied in appearance by the ocean. If we may credit history and tradition, whole parishes have been swept away.'

Armstrong was confident that marram would sort out the matter. He wrote:

It grows upon the very driest land upon the sea shore, and it prevents the wind carrying the land from the shore, and dispersing it over the adjoining fields.... Many a fertile acre hath been covered with unprofitable land and rendered entirely useless, which might have been prevented by sowing the seeds of this plant upon the shore.

The vicar of Horsey, William Ivory, contributed a letter to Armstrong's publication about the coastal erosion, and his information adds useful details of damage done between Waxham and Winterton:

The present bad effects of these breaches are the salt water and the sands destroy all the products of a number of acres of marshes, and every tide, if it should happen that the wind should blow very briskly in the north-west, the sea, by that means being much increased, it would drown all the low country, even as far as Norwich.

Armstrong spends several pages of his text explaining that an ancient Act of Parliament and also appeals to the county justices had failed to achieve anything. To really drive his point home, he quotes the 1609 Act, which was supposed to apply a 'speedy recovery of many thousand acres of marsh ground ... within the counties of Norfolk and Suffolk' and then lists the towns and parishes affected by breaks on to land by the sea – seventy-six in Norfolk and sixteen in Suffolk.

He also appends notes on specific events and places, and there is even a personal note: the man has been and seen, not merely written from the comfort of his study.

Since this little memoir went to press, I have observed the sea-breaches on the eastern coast near Horsey; but the weather being very unfavourable (Wednesday, 27 July 1791) and the land of the Mill-Banks flooded, I could not, without great personal danger, pass.

He was right to locate one of the remedies against erosion to be such methods of binding soil and sand into root systems. As geologists have often pointed out, East Anglia is always in a state of mutability. As geologist Richard Fortey put it in his study of landscape, 'The land is literally blowing away.' He continues, 'In dry weather the peat turns into light, dry granules that can be whipped into a dust storm by a strong wind. There are few hedges in such ranch-land to stop this deflation.'

The 1890s also saw some of the worst weather on this coast. One correspondent to *The Standard* wrote from sea-oppressed Eccles with some alarming facts:

Sir,
The temperature here seems to have been lower than anything I have seen published in the last few days. I have a Negretti and Zambra maximum and minimum thermometer hung in the porch of my house, facing south, and sheltered from the easterly and northerly winds; yet last Monday evening at nine o'clock it marked five degrees F, or thirty degrees of frost. The river Thet was frozen from bank to bank.

On the southern fringe of The Wash there is much deposition of materials, and so the salt marshes grow. The historical record shows plenty of encroachment on property. In 1928, there was a typical report on the process, on this occasion at Hunstanton, with the grand heading of 'Neptune's Inroads':

The back gardens of the nearest houses are now only 5 yards from the water. For some distance, large quantities of earth have been washed into the sea and the slanting ground cut away, leaving a steep back. Nearly 100 houses and bungalows are in the danger area.

Storms and floods

There is also the subject of the rate of loss regarding the land on shore and cliff. In most parts of the land, antiquarians and various amateurs with a passion for local history spent a great deal of time trying to log the amount of land lost to erosion. In Yorkshire, for instance, Thomas Sheppard meticulously recorded rates of sea encroachment. Norfolk was no different in this. In 1845, the great geologist Charles Lyell studied the situation at Sheringham, and this was reported in *The Times*:

Mr Lyell makes a remarkable statement respecting Sheringham ... he ascertained in 1829 some facts which throw light upon the rate at which the sea gains upon the land. It was computed, when the present inn was built in 1805, that it would require seventy years for the sea to reach the spot, the mean loss of land being calculated from previous operations to be somewhat less than one yard annually. The distance between the house and the sea was 50 yards but no allowance was made for the slope of the ground being from the sea, in consequence of which the waste was naturally accelerated every year as the cliff grew lower. ... Between the years 1824 and 1829, no less than 17 yards were swept away.

Estimations such as this were being made in all kinds of places, and aims varied between open scaremongering and supposedly accurate scientific reporting.

Of course, the storms and floods caused inundations into the rivers running out from The Wash as well. In 1862, the Middle Levels flooded – the waterways between the rivers Nene and Great Ouse. This was in late October, and *The Illustrated London News* provided a number of very impressive illustrations of damage done. Their feature 'Disastrous Gale' was the kind of report that was all too frequent throughout the nineteenth century:

On Saturday, about noon, the wind gradually got up from the south-west, and with heavy rain, continued to increase until late in the evening. ... Ships and steamers are afloat all down the east coast. Tynemouth, South Shields, Scarborough, Great Yarmouth and Lowestoft report disasters, and there is no doubt we have suffered one of the most severe and destructive gales which has visited us in late years.

The Norfolk estuary attracted many theories and projected schemes from individuals and organisations, and this was all about both navigation and inundation. The inherent problems may be seen in the parliamentary enquiry led by Lord Camperdown, which closed in 1876. There was opposition to schemes suggested, most notably by the Prince of Wales, represented by his brief, General Knollys, because damage had been done to land on the Sandringham estate. There had even been a plan to make a new English county, a piece of land created by making a massive embankment on The Wash. But the Norfolk Estuary Company, with its grand designs, was in trouble by the time of the enquiry, although it had created a navigable cut extending over 2 miles and even diverted a river. This company now pleaded for backing and for more powers to act; the Pilot and Harbour Commissioners for King's Lynn were against the company's plans, and so the enquiry was playing a vital part in settling the matter.

Influential men

Vested interests won the day, and as usual, matters were adjourned, although conclusions given were well argued. There were ongoing disputes and discussions in the eighteenth century as efforts began to be made to improve drainage and do something about the silted harbours. At times, the greatest engineers of the day were called to give their opinion. At Wells-next-the-Sea, the magistrates called on John Smeaton, the famous engineer and lighthouse builder, to give evidence regarding how the port would be affected by the embankments at the Slade marshes. Smeaton was his usual thorough self, giving very detailed information and opinion. He was keen to stress that all his observations were based on his own experience: there was nothing too nebulously theoretical about Smeaton. The occasion was the first recorded instance of a court using an 'expert witness' – and this was in 1782, although he had made observations on the area long before.

Smeaton's comments tell us a lot about the basis of sound knowledge among proper scientists at the time with reference to the action and threat of water. For instance, he was well aware of the problems created by jetties – structures that many thought would protect shores, later in the nineteenth century. Smeaton's opinion was:

> I entirely disapprove of all jetties built into the stream, as a defence for saving the banks and foreshores from the action of water, as I am convinced from my observations that they have a directly contrary tendency; for they seldom fail of producing a deep pit either opposite to or on the downstream side of the jetty, which tends to undermine the banks, and even the jetty itself, so that thereby the rent is made worse.

He felt it necessary also to comment on the main problem facing the North Norfolk men: flooding. He had worked on the Grand Sluice over The Haven, which had put an end to the regular flooding of the Boston and Lincoln area. Smeaton had worked with John Grundy from Spalding, and Langley Edwards, a King's Lynn man who had been involved in the navigation projects on the Nar and Blyth. Smeaton had endless knowledge based on practical encounters with the threat of the sea, and he told the magistrates, 'I do not know of any security against inundations in a county that is defended by banks, otherwise than by making these banks not only sufficiently strong but high enough to sustain the greatest extremes without being overflown.'

He had useful local contacts, and he knew Langley Edwards; they were both aware of the adverse effects of marshes, and the desirability of shifting them. Edwards had written, with reference to the Grand Sluice, that it would be:

> a great addition to the health of all inhabitants of the circumjacent city, towns and villages, by removing the cause of these noxious vapours which must arise from stagnant waters and which by the various actions of the winds, are wafted to the nostrils of those who are seated within reach thereof.

Consequently, there were more than just the engineering issues up for debate here: public health was a factor in all considerations involving water. The sea rushed in, and much of it could not recede; embankment followed, in order to create workable land, followed in turn by stagnation, with all the usual marshland insects. With hindsight, the health issues are so plainly predictable. Writing in 1891, 'a Lynn sexagenarian' gives us an insight into this subject:

> I heard the late Mr Byles (afterwards Mr Justice Byles) in a cause at the Town Hall. What the occasion was I forget, but no doubt it was about drainage (a very prolific source of controversy and litigation) and there was a great deal said in the course of the proceedings about a 'puddle bank'.

The same writer also provides us with a summary of some of the main changes happening at King's Lynn during his life: if we say that he was in his teens in about 1845, then his summary covers the second half of the century:

> We had two ship-building yards here: one at the North end, belonging to Mr Larkin; and another in the Friars, occupied by Mr Richardson. From these I have seen vessels of 300 to 400 tons launched. We had also a tobacco factory, carried on by Mr Cyprian Hilton, afterwards by Mr Edward Pindar. … The Hiltons lived in St Ann's Street, where the tobacco factory then was. … There was also a paper mill near the South Gates, carried on by Messrs Munn of Thetford. All these industries are now extinct.

At that time, when the above writer was a mature man, the town had largely erased most of the troubles caused by the maritime incursions. A guidebook of 1875 explains, regarding the results of the advancing sea meeting the outflow of the Great Ouse:

> The town is about 4m. From the outfall of the river, and 10m. From the open sea, called Lynn Deeps; the intervening space or 'wash' being occupied by vast sand and mud banks, and formerly navigable only through intricate channels. But these evils have been corrected by the construction of a new and direct channel.

A new dock had also been opened, in 1869.

The Norfolk around The Wash and the great rivers Nene and Ouse is a marshland, and through that there has always been a network of what locals term the old 'green roads'. In the voluminous library of memoirs concerning this area, there is ample evidence of the importance of these elements of life. The poacher who is the subject of Lilias Rider Haggard's countryside classic *I Walked by Night*, for instance, knew the place close up, and he explained the importance of the green roads to the coast:

> My old grandfather have told me that the smugglers used all these green roads and by-ways to smuggle their contraband goods, and that

they had their holes and hidden places all along these routes. Where I was a keeper we had a very large warren beside the road running from Wormagay. One day the warreners were digging at the bottom of a large hill … and they came on a large hole about 4 yards square, which it was plain to see had been all timbered up many years before. A gentleman came and looked at it and said it was one of the smugglers' holes.

It cannot be stressed too much just how tightly knit the hinterlands of The Wash and the life on the coast has always been. The communications have been marked and well used since Roman times or even earlier. Travelling around Hunstanton and Castle Rising today, for instance, one remarkable feature of the land is the preponderance of little villages and hamlets huddled around the lanes. In spite of the agricultural character around there, one may still sense the presence of this place where a network of walking paths was established and exploited. It is no accident that Walsingham and its famous shrine, along with the Pilgrims' Way, stands in the very heart of this northern stretch of the county.

The story of the sea's threat is dramatically explained with reference to the continuing flood problems. As I write this in 2016, the Environment Agency is listing flood warnings around the area, giving specific details for towns and villages along the rivers.

In 1863, a railway guide gave the essence of King's Lynn, which is, of course, the very heart of this part of Norfolk:

It is divided into several parts by four small rivers, called fleets, and was formerly encompassed on the land side by a foss, defended by a wall and bastions. The harbour is difficult of entrance, but capable of receiving 300 sail of vessels.

King's Lynn, as shown by the magistrates' need of advice and knowledge from Smeaton, was confronted, for a very long time, with all kinds of problems regarding the encroachment of the sea as marsh and bog. Writing about the port, Norfolk historian Neil Storey explained that it had its great heyday: 'The wealth of the port in 1374 is reflected in the fact that Lynn sent nineteen ships, when Ipswich only provided twelve and Harwich fourteen for Edward III's expedition to France.' The cause of the decline, which went with the actions of the sea, was a result of the draining of the Fens by Dutch engineer Cornelius Vermuyden in the seventeenth century; drainage in one area had caused silting in others, and Lynn was the recipient of the obstructions of silt. When Daniel Defoe came in the 1720s, he commented that the town was 'rich and populous and thriving', and Defoe added that the tradesmen of Lynn dealt with 'about six counties wholly and three counties in part'. Taking a wider picture, and bringing in the Glaven Ports as a whole, he noted that over twenty years (1700–20), the number of ships travelling yearly down to London had doubled.

In the period 1860–80, however, as previously noted, new docks were built – the Alexandra first, and then the Bentinck, so again, King's Lynn could cope with much larger ships. But as Neil Storey points out, not everyone was happy. The fishermen saw their fleet cut by half, and they were clinging on to their old ways of working. Storey wrote, explaining trouble during the building of the dock: 'When a boom was placed across the fleet the workmen and observing councillors had to be protected by policemen.'

The first official Royal Commission and early maps

In 1911, the Royal Commission on Coastal Erosion included a detailed survey of the East Anglian coast. The summary this gives for the line of coast from Lynn to Wells, and their explanation of the process of accretion, is helpful in understanding the accumulation of marshland that everywhere meets the eye:

> The lower greensand and the Drift beds that fringe it are here separated from The Wash by a strip of low alluvial land, down to the neighbourhood of Hunstanton Station, and along the northern part of this, the alluvium, in its turn, is bordered and protected by a strip of shingle.

The same writer comments that 'along this somewhat peculiar coast there have probably been many changes in shore deposits, as may be seen by a comparison of the new Ordnance map with the old one.'

This is the ideal point at which to introduce this element of the mapping of this area, as this is a simple and visual way to see the losses from the coast. For the comparison suggested, the map produced by Thomas Milne in 1797 provides excellent visual knowledge of the coast. This map was published and overseen by William Faden, although Milne and his assistants did the actual work in producing it. Faden was geographer to King George III and had premises in London. He lived at a time when the Royal Society was encouraging the production of maps. In 1784, for instance, a map of Suffolk had been produced by Joseph Hodskinson. Faden contacted the Royal Society after his work had been done on Norfolk, hoping to win a gold medal. That never happened, but at least we have a map that shows very strongly and neatly the nature of the Norfolk coast, with some hints about land lost or gained.

There was a map extant in Faden's time: a War Office map produced in 1793, but J.C. Barringer, writing on the Faden/Milne map, explains that, 'It is incomplete. ... All greens and commons are clearly shown but many other details had obviously not been plotted.'

Throughout my accounts of the coastal locations, I refer to Milne's map, and there are limitations, as Barringer explains in this comment: 'It is doubtful ... if we can trust Faden's surveyors' measurements sufficiently to be able to assess the rate of erosion of the cliffs at Overstrand since 1797.' Nevertheless, it is all we have.

In this instance, moving along the south bank of The Wash from Hunstanton, we reach Wells-next-the-Sea. The Faden map, when compared to the beach today, shows a tidal area, not the holiday centre we have now. There could not be a clearer instance of the accretion of land here. Wells, according to local historian Roger Arguile, was a small fishing port through medieval times, but was thriving and of some importance. He explains, 'Local fishermen turned to cod and to Iceland,' and writes that 'by 1357, there was an active cod industry.' As usual with all these ports along The Wash, drainage was a recurring problem. A map of 1789 makes it clear that there had been a number of efforts to dig channels for sluicing, but that everything in that way had been piecemeal and incomplete. In this situation, Wells needed a sound, solid harbour, and eventually there was one. Roger Arguile explains that eventually the commerce with London was to be one of Wells' most successful enterprises through its history. The key crop was barley, hence the appearance of the huge and distinctive barley storage barns on the landscape.

The railway arrived in 1857, when the line from East Dereham was established at Wells with the usual extension. It was destined to be yet another popular holiday destination and that is a success story. But with regard to the enemy, the sea, flooding has always been the threat. Roger Arguile gives a very explicit account of the origin of the floods: 'If coupled with strong northerly winds, a tidal surge down the narrowing length of the North Sea exposes the Norfolk Coast to sudden and severe flooding.' He adds that in the crisis year of 1953, 'In Wells, the west bank of the channel was breached in three places.'

Chapter 4

Norfolk's North Sea Coast

Run sand scooped from the soft cliffs of Norfolk through your hands: as in an hourglass, this is ephemeral time. Will humankind endure longer than these cliffs, which crumble daily into the indifferent sea?

Richard Fortey, *The Hidden Landscape*

Enter Mr Hewitt

One of the most detailed studies of the advance of the North Sea on this coast was undertaken by William Hewitt in 1844. Like so many other writers, Mr Hewitt had a cunning plan to defeat the waves and tides. This involved two items that were to be in the forefront of attempts to combat the actions of the sea for the succeeding years, right up to the present day: marram grass and groynes. Hewitt's long essay gives a very clear idea of the issues and problems involved along this coast, and he not only names places but also particular people who had land at various spots. His overall survey explains very powerfully the nature of the task facing anyone with bright ideas about solving the problems:

> From the earliest records to the present time, that portion of coast extending from Cromer to Winterton-ness has been most subject to the ravages of the ocean; lands have been swept away, buildings of considerable value have been swallowed up, and notwithstanding every effort hitherto made, the sea continues to advance in the interior as little satiated as before.... The Hasborough Sands, extending from Winterton, to or a little beyond Bacton, must ... be a source of considerable mischief, confining a vast body of water within a narrow limit, which, when increased and disturbed by gales of wind from the north-west, upon a spring tide, urges the waves against the cliffs.

It is almost as if he is taking all this personally, and as if the sea is angry Nature personified.

Hewitt gives the reader some startling facts to drive home his concern for this coast: 'The whole site of ancient Cromer now forms part of the German Ocean, the inhabitants having gradually retreated inland to the present situation, from whence the sea still threatens to dislodge them.' He also refers to Trimingham, not far from Cromer, as being subject to incursions, and then, referring to Mundesley he specifically talks about 'the property belonging to Mr Wheatley' and this, he reports, 'has become considerably reduced in extent and value, and has only been preserved by substantial walls erected next the sea, and numerous piles of wood driven into the sand beyond them.'

The tract also points out that 'the ancient villages of Shipden, Whimpwell and Keswick have entirely disappeared,' and regarding Eccles, whose story is told later in this chapter, he notes, 'A monument, however, still remains in the tower of the old church, which is half buried in the sand.' Of course, Hewitt backs this up by referring to the forces of the sands and the frequent storms as well, and chooses 1792 as the year in which one of the worst incursions took place: 'a body of water passed through between Horsey and Waxham, extending beyond Hickling, a village situated 3 miles inland, which uniting with the fresh water contained in a large lake, destroyed all the fish.'

Mr Hewitt's answer is marram grass and groynes. He moves on to these topics after explaining that there are sediments collecting in other places and so land is created as other land is destroyed. He includes in this the cockle sands off Caister, which he notes 'have increased since 1836 one mile and a half in extent to the northward'. In order to drive home his point of the sheer desperation of the Norfolk people on this coast, he again refers to Mr Wheatley, who had used the hulls of old ships on the shore by his property, filling the hulls with large stones, but this was futile: 'a few years since they were entirely removed by the sea during a heavy gale.' In writing on Cromer he shows an understanding of the accumulation of sand as another threat, recalling that the jetty was eventually brought down and the local people began to understand that the location of such things as groynes or jetties was the important factor.

But Hewitt still sees a combination of piers, groynes and grass as the solution. Wooden groynes have been in use since the 1720s, and they are effective, but there are limitations in their use. At Mappleton, on the Yorkshire coast, for instance, rock groynes were installed in 1991 and this stopped materials being moved along and lost in that location, but this had the effect of increasing erosion further south.

Hewitt argued in his publication that prototype groynes put in place at Trimingham had failed, even though planks had been fixed by iron bolts, and blamed this failure on the lack of a deep embedding in the sands.

Further up the east coast, in Yorkshire, similar experiments with groynes were underway; there is an account of Withernsea in an old journal, and there the groynes are given a special mention:

A stroll on the seashore, when the waves are rolling mighty billows on to the sands and washing away the clay cliffs, demonstrates forcibly the irresistible power of the ocean. Stand on the pier at Withernsea, when the wind is strong from the east, and the sight is grand. The water rolls up in great hills and valleys with a majestic sweep, curls in crescents of foam, dashing the spray high up in the air ... and roars with a sullen sound, as if angry that its advances are repelled by the 'groins' [sic] that withstand its devastations. The 'groins' are formed of piles driven deep into the sand and clay, strong planks connecting the piles. The 'groins' are carried out in a straight line towards the low-water mark. They are placed about 100 yards apart and are effectual not only in helping to uphold the base of the clay cliffs, but gather an accumulation of the shifting sands.

Groynes at that time were not always the solution: the British weather saw to that. In 1867 in Whitstable, as one press report commented, 'great injury was done to the shores by the washing away of the groins and beach.'

The Victorian writers were struggling to understand the action of sand and gravel with regard to the use of groynes, and there were numerous publications on the sands, as there were on tides, as the science of geology gained momentum since its early and rather piecemeal predecessors, the antiquaries of the Enlightenment. When it came to the topic of groynes and piers, they began to use their knowledge of how the tides worked on the beach deposits.

A major factor, they started to see, in the working of erosion, is the phenomenon of longshore drift. This refers to the process of moving materials on a beach due to the angular movement of the waves coming on to the beach. The gradient of a beach affects that regular oblique wave movement and a severe storm can affect the whole process. Usually, the normal rate of erosion happens when the movement of beach material is caused by the waves coming at an angle. Their force forwards, called the swash, is followed by the recession – the backwash. This makes a shingle beach last only so long; the backwash and longshore drift takes it along, following the course of the oblique tide. This is how the lost pebbles and mud from the Yorkshire cliffs gradually shift along to Spurn to form a main shingle belt. This knowledge opened up the question of how attempts to stay the action of the tide in one place tended to cause problems elsewhere. To add to the frustration, groynes need constant repair and reinforcement as well.

The explanation in geological terms, by a professional, also helps here. This describes longshore drift as being something related to the wind direction: on coasts of an unstable nature, sand tends to be drawn away and so cliffs are exposed. As one geologist has explained, 'The long-term result of this sensitivity to cliff line orientation is that the whole coast is gradually attempting to develop a shape that lies at right angles to the predominantly north-easterly wave direction.'

Thomas Sheppard, a geologist who actually walked the land he wrote about, carefully gives an account of Withernsea's land loss over the nineteenth century and earlier, but he starts with the groynes: 'Opposite the village-or town-of Withernsea, the groynes, since their erection in 1870, have been helpful in preserving the seafront, and the promenade in more recent years has also assisted, as doubtless will the extension thereto just completed.' He noted the greater loss of land south of Withernsea itself, and that is exactly what happened in the Mappleton example:

Just south of Withernsea, there is a sudden and great increase in the breadth of the strip of land lost since 1852 and the Geological Surveyors found the coast had so altered in this part of Holderness that they had the 'new coast of 1881' engraved for their map instead of following the usual custom of putting their work on the old Ordnance Survey sheets.

The topic of groynes and their usefulness continued to attract discussion and debate well into the twentieth century. But even in the Edwardian years, most commentators saw the advantages of groynes, as in this feature from the *Sheffield Daily Telegraph* in 1904:

> The earlier heavy timber groynes, consisting of timber frames filled with chalk, proved fairly effective in breaking the force of the waves, but were too high to have proper effect in causing accretion on the foreshore. The later construction of four long low timber groynes however had the result of causing, within three years the accumulation of 500,000 tons of sand on the foreshore, raising the beach to an average height of about 4 feet over an area of 25,000 square yards.

Over the century since that feature, the same kind of groynes have been retained, but often backed by netted rock revetments, as has been done at Humberston, for instance. There, on the coast looking directly across to the Spurn Head, the incoming tides are swift and ruthless, and even with modern technology and meteorology, there has to be constant vigilance on the low cliffs above the beaches.

Hewitt looked to the positive in his suggestions for a remedy. He saw that the outstanding feature of the East Anglian coast in terms of what was attacked and what was preserved often depended on the gathering of sandbanks across river estuaries. He selects Yarmouth to explain:

> In Yarmouth the sea has not advanced upon the sands in the slightest degree since the reign of Elizabeth, and where the town is built became firm and habitable ground about the year 1008, from which time a line of dunes has gradually increased in height and breadth.

A very clear instance of the sort of place that was once a port but is now a 'curious little village', can be gleaned from the words of the energetic traveller

H.V. Morton, who walked this way in the early 1920s. In his account of his time there, he stops at Stiffkey, and writes:

> It is a curious little village noted for its cockle women. I went down to the long sea marsh. I crossed rotting timbers flung across creeks and I went for miles through mud and marsh till I came at length to a distant ridge of sand which has wrecked more ships than the Needles, and the incredible expanse of shore.

He gives one of the most vivid descriptions of this part of the coast, and concludes with a thought about the marshes that evokes its timeless appeal:

> This is a curious part of the world ... a region rich in history and packed full of atmosphere. You can stand on the salt marshes towards the end of the day, with the sun mellow over the windy fields of sea lavender, and it takes little to imagine the Viking ships beaching on the distant strand.

Glaven Ports and others

This is the point at which to look at the so-called Glaven ports, before moving on to the string of places along the coast below. These are Cley, Wiveton and Blakeney. Over a century ago, W.A. Dutt described this area vividly:

> Beyond Sheringham the cliffs soon give place to the Weybourne flats and Salthouses, Cley and Blakeney salt marshes, which lie between those picturesque villages and the sea, intersected by saltwater creeks and the shallow, winding channels by which small coasting craft make their way up to Cley and Blakeney quays.

The ports take their name from the river Glaven, which is prone to being blocked up by the movement of the spit of shingle here.

At the heart of the area is Blakeney Point, now a nature reserve, which is primarily composed of dunes and a shingle and sand spit, managed by the National Trust since 1912. It may now attract primarily naturalists and walkers, but for many centuries this was a habitable place. There was a monastery here, and a place that was most likely a home for someone, referred to as Blakeney Chapel, lies beneath the marshland. As usual with North Norfolk, it has been the long series of reclamation schemes that has resulted in the stagnation marsh development and the loss of dwelling places.

Blakeney is part of Cley, and there has been steady expansion of the spit, contrasting with the loss of land at Cley. Today the coastal path meets the Peddar's Way path, an ancient road that starts at Blackwater on the Little Ouse and goes to Holme on the coast. As its end at the coast is close to what was a Roman *castellum*, a fortified signal station, at Brancaster. There is no doubt that this is a very old pathway.

It became a nature reserve in 1912, home for all kinds of wading birds and seals, and in the mudflats there is naturally a plethora of molluscs and crustaceans. This is a vast tract of wetland, shingle and salt marsh. The spit at Blakeney is several miles long. It has a base of shingle, on which, in some places, plants such as sea lavender and poppies have grown, so although the spit is constantly moving, and partly being eroded, the plant life is helping to make some degree of stability.

In the great floods of 1953, Blakeney was one of the places that took some of the worst inundations. Robert Macfarlane, the writer who knows the area very well, explained in his book *The Wild Places* what the background was to that terrible freak of nature:

> The surge struck the North Norfolk coast first. Blakeney Point was immediately overwhelmed, the Cley marshes flooded, and the Holkham pines stood in water. Warning should have been sent south, but in the chaos it was not, and a short time later, the sea-defences along the Essex coast were swamped. The sea wall was breached in dozens of places.

The friary at Blakeney, founded in 1296, was dissolved with so many others in the Dissolution of the monasteries in the time of Henry VIII. The place referred to as the Chapel was a place of higher ground with a surrounding ditch; there were people there – on and off – until the seventeenth century. As with many small ports on the east coast, Blakeney had its period of importance regarding naval and military operations, such as the part it played in the campaigns of Edward I against the Scots in 1301. This status continued into the Tudor period, when it was important enough to merit having a customs house. There are theories that Blakeney church was important too, being used as a beacon, but that may be questioned.

There are many accounts of actually sailing in this area, but one of the most vivid is from the pen of the famous artist Edward Seago, whose book *Tideline* includes this account of the difficulties inherent in a world of shingle and mud-banks:

> I had always imagined that, once outside the harbour mouth, one pointed the ship in a certain direction and went places. But I was wrong. It is just as difficult to cruise about the sea as it is to drive around the country. There are just as many highways and by-ways, but they are called channels, and it's a hundred times more difficult because they are invisible.

Seago has given us some of the most evocative and accurate images of this country, from his *Breydon Mud*, which shows huge groynes among the silt, with long bridges behind, to *Misty Morning, Brancaster*, which shows four boats moored in a sea fret, showing Brancaster's ability to imbue the traveller with a sense of wonder equal to the best writing of the Romantic poets. He can also depict the threat of the sea, as in his *The Beach at Palling*, in which a flimsy wooden fence of interconnected groynes seems to stand at the mercy of the waves, with vaguely present cliffs in the distance.

One of the most vivid and powerful accounts of this few square miles of coast comes from the late Roger Deakin, whose great bestseller of 2007, *Wildwood*, includes a chapter devoted to a trip out to Scolt Head, off Norton Creek, with its western headland sticking out into Brancaster Bay. Deakin went out with friends through the Brancaster marshes, the spur to this being the news that some parts of an ancient wood had emerged on Holme Beach. Deakin and friends settle in a hut out on this wild coast. They have a book by an academic expert with them, together with a plentiful supply of tea, and what they find is something much more recent – a relic of the Second World War: 'Harry finds part of a gun-turret. I kick away the sand and reveal the cellular structure of a wing.' What comes from Deakin's journeys around that area is the fact that, aside from any lost villages along Norfolk's coast, there is also the inescapable conclusion that the twentieth-century wars have left their debris also. After all, in the Great War, Zeppelin airship-bombers flew this way, and in the war with Nazi Germany, all kinds of military emplacements were sited along the east coast.

Nearby Cley has had an eventful history regarding its relationship with the sea. In the early seventeenth century, after reclamation work, the Glaven channel was silted and the wharf at Cley had to be moved. Cley declined, in spite of the employment of the great engineer Thomas Telford in the 1820s. As the traveller Arthur Mee wrote about Cley, almost a century ago, 'Its greatness is gone, though some of its glory remains, and barrows on the heather uplands stir the imagination with the thought of ancestors of Norfolk folk 3,000 years ago.' Mee also described the customs house: 'red brick with Georgian windows ... the *maison de quai* has walls of brick and cobble.' The church really impressed him, provoking him to write, 'There is nothing lovelier here than the south porch, with its traceried battlements, and a beautiful niche and windows over an entrance arch adorned with flowers and shields.' But the church has been the focus of interest in much more recent times.

Matthew Champion reported on a project in 2016 that looked at the medieval graffiti there; he wrote, 'Medieval vessels can still be found in Cley, though sailing across the stonework of its church walls in one of East Anglia's finest collections of ship graffiti.' He explained that these images range from drawings of shipping vessels to elaborate carvings of craft. Champion also wrote about 'ritual protection marks, builders' accounts, images of long-dead parishioners and one of the most unusual inscriptions found to date in any Norfolk church'. This is a *mappa mundi*, a world map. Of all the categories of remains and evidences of past life in this area, this is surely one of the most unusual and the most enlightening.

Regarding the Peddar's Way, which reaches to this coastal area, there have been some remarkable insights into the nature of the routes followed by the cattlemen and drovers in the historical record, and few of these have been so vivid and lively as the tales uncovered by that indefatigable oral historian, George Ewart Evans. In his account of the cattle trade and the Norwich drovers, he explains that down the years there has been an international and cross-country trade here. One of his correspondents told him, 'I started droving with my father in 1908 or 1909. The cattle came from the ports by railway to Trowse station in Norwich. D'you know, they'd take only about fourteen hours from Holyhead?' Evans found out that thirty-five wagons of cattle would come to Norwich, from various parts of Ireland, and then be sold on across the county. One drover told him, 'Our job after the sale was over was to walk the cattle to the farmers who'd bought them; and we'd have up to 200 cattle on the road of a Sunday morning. ... We used to go out to North Walsham, Dereham and so on.'

If we put together this kind of droving, within one limited range of land, with the older history of the great tracks such as the Peddar's Way, it takes little effort to see that such activities would extend to the coastal villages. In other words, the networks across the county have surely always extended far from the immediate local areas where the most important populated centres have been developed.

It is impossible to leave out Hunstanton in any account of the encroachment of the sea and other forms of erosion. There have certainly been storms and floods there. One of the most remarkable in its history was the events of 31 January 1953, the year when so many east coast places were swamped. On this occasion around 10 feet of seawater flooded the lower South Beach part of town; there were at the time a number of United States service people billeted there, and the storm and flood brought a heroic story.

This was about Reis Leming, who was based with the 67th Air Rescue Squadron. Reis went out into the dark night, wading in the deep water, and succeeded in saving twenty-seven people, keeping on working until he was exhausted. He clearly made an impact on the local community, and even though he returned to the United States after the war, it was Hunstanton women who baked his wedding cake when he held his wedding in the town. Later he was given the award of the American Soldier's Medal by his country. He was an aerial gunner – a very risky business – but on that night he made his courage tell in a very different sphere of activity.

Hunstanton and shipwrecks have always gone together. The long chronicle of maritime disasters off that coast is a depressing succession of gales and wrecks, with desperate attempts to save lives. Even one of the local myths involves a wreck: the tale that is told regarding the fragment of St Edmund's chapel by the lighthouse. The legend is that in the time before Edmund became king of what was then, in Saxon times, East Anglia, he was very nearly shipwrecked there, and he founded the chapel as a thanks to divine providence that he lived to tell the tale.

In 1809, Francis Blomefield, in his voluminous account of the whole county of Norfolk, gave a succinct account of Hunstanton's situation regarding the sea raging at its door:

> Hunstanton Lordship stands at the north-east point of Norfolk where it is washed by the great German Ocean, and is remarkable for its lofty cliff, about 100 feet high, against which the raging sea comes with such force and fury, that it is supposed to have gained by length of time, a considerable tract of land, about 2 miles; the strata of this cliff ... are worthy of consideration; under the surface which is about 2 or 3 feet deep, lies a strong white chalk, then a red hard clunch stone, below that a stone of a yellow colour, and the lowest stratum is exceeding durable ... yet it is said that sometimes, in great storms ... the sea surmounts all.
>   [Note: clunch being chalky, limestone rock.]

Blomefield understood the geology, and his description shows that he sees the name of the topmost, recent rock, with its vulnerability to weathering. The crucial phrase, though, is 'the sea ... surmounts all'.

In the 1911 Royal Commission report, the geologist who inspected the Hunstanton area wrote:

> we have a cliff ... with boulder clay at the southern end, but mainly Lower Greensand, which sips down out of sight at the northern end. The last bed makes a firm base and runs out along the foreshore as a rocky mass. ... The chalk, too, is fairly hard and I saw nothing but very slight falls from the cliff.

Today, the visitor to Old Hunstanton can see nothing but wide sands backed at the coast by sand dunes where beach huts predominate on the landscape. It is ideal for windsurfing and dog walking, and the place retains all the essential qualities of the traditional English seaside. The most striking feature regarding those cliffs is their colour: the sharp contrast in the two main strata – white and orange – being a combination of carrstone (a sandstone) and chalk.

Seahenge

In this part of the county, on the southern edge of The Wash, there has been one of the most exciting archaeological finds on record: that of so-called Seahenge, at Holme-next-the-Sea. This is a Bronze Age timber circle, found in 1998. Obviously, after its discovery there was a lot more study of it undertaken. When it was created, it would have been placed in what was a salt marsh. The circle was composed of fifty-five posts with a diameter of 6.6 metres; the posts would have been 3 metres high. The first photograph taken at the site shows the posts with a central block, which was actually a tree stump.

As Nicholas Crane commented in his book *Coast*, 'We'll never know exactly what moved a community to erect an oak ring on the salt marsh that once connected their woods and pastures to Doggerland.' But with the help of dendrochronology (tree-ring dating), we do know that the circle was made in the spring or summer of 2049 BC.

Studies have shown that the wood indicates that over fifty axes were at work on Seahenge. This was clearly a find that needed special treatment, and the wood was moved to Flag Fen in Cambridgeshire to be treated with preservatives, and then shifted again, down to the experts who worked on the *Mary Rose* timbers at Portsmouth Historic Dockyard. Speculation will go on regarding what the purpose of this structure was, and one suggestion, by the writer of the website for the Norfolk Museums Collections, is that 'perhaps the body of a high-ranking person may have been placed on the upturned stump to be picked clean by animals and birds.'

Holidaymakers along the coast down from here are always likely to come across the stunted trunk bases of other areas of this ancient forest, and such sights give the visitor the very smallest clue as to what was there so long ago, when there was a land bridge to Europe.

My Survey

It is impossible to resist, at this point, a quote. This is a traditional rhyme about the Norfolk Coast communities:

> *Cromer crabs*
> *Runton dabs*
> *Beeston babies*
> *Sheringham ladies*
> *Weybourne witches*
> *Cley bitches*
> *Salthouse ditches*
> *Langham fairmaids*
> *Blakeney bulldogs*
> *Morston doddermen*
> *Binham bulls*
> *Wells bite-fingers*
> *And the Blakeney people*
> *Stand on the steeple and crack hazelnuts*
> *With a five-farthing beetle*

It would take a real folklore expert with local knowledge to decipher this, but one thing behind these lines that is relevant here is that the folk of Blakeney were clearly, in past times, thought of as being vulnerable, and strangely open to gentle teasing. But a *dodderman* being a snail, it seems that those dwellers were open to fun as well. Polly Howat, in her *Tales of Old Norfolk*, comments on the Wells reference: 'One of the inhabitants of Wells is reported to have bitten off the finger of a drowned sailor in order to get his ring.'

With all this as a context or the story of the lost places, what follows is an account of the coastal communities between Weybourne and Gorleston. At times my story may touch on such matters as legend, hearsay and oral history, but essentially, this is a checklist of what has been lost. These disappeared places were centre stage in 2012, when a photographic exhibition was staged in Waxham Great Barn called 'The Raging Sea: Norfolk's Lost Villages'. David Stannard, who was involved in the project, told the press, ' If you go down on to the beach on Saturday evening when it is getting dark and there is the ruin of a church and a circle of flints in the sand, you can only think, "How did this happen?"' He explained that he and his friends found 'foundations, cart tracks in the clay, Roman pottery, skeletons in graves … and these wells'. This refers to the gradual emergence into view of eleven wells from 1986 to 1996.

A map of the coast of this stretch has been compiled for the *Victoria County History of Norfolk*, and there, as drawn in 1906, the small coastal settlements of 1086 are marked. Most are easily placed with the present names, but notably, Eccles is located on the edge, as it were; there is some land marked between the sea and 'Wintretuna' (Winterton) and also between 'Hemesbei' (Hemsby) and the sea.

Weybourne

In the scenic little community of Weybourne, the heritage identity meets the powerful brooding presence of the sea. At the beach, the track of the Norfolk coast path is cut and the shingle dominates, tractored into high ridges as the main strategy to keep out the sea's rush. The beach shingle is framed on both sides by the soft cliffs, sinking into sand, liquefying inexorably, as I am now entirely accustomed to seeing. A close-up of the cliff reveals the soft, sandy earth with occasional great pockmarks, which turn out to be the rocks of flint, with their black, blue and white markings seeming almost like some kind of template for domestic design.

Walking these shingle beaches, every step is laboured and purposeful; the crunch beneath your feet is a sharp yet full sound, like an element of percussion in the orchestration of coastal sounds. The sea lies much lower down in its deep basin, lying like some great sleeping creature, while before it, humans and dogs move deliberately around.

A mile the other side of the village is the railway station of the North Norfolk Line. My visit there coincided with the imminent arrival of a train and the enthusiasts were gathered. The station buildings were bright brown and yellow, their paint seeming fresh and clean in the September sun. I enjoyed a mug of strong tea, inspected the railway bookstall, and chatted with Roy, the stationmaster. He was keen to tell me that the *Black Prince*, an especially beautiful engine, was being hosed down as we spoke, so I glanced at the strong machine, dominant in the sheds area as some prize bull at a farm.

This was, and still is, part of the ongoing railway facility for what many call the 'Royal Coast' because, of course, Sandringham is just around the corner. Roy joked about the Midland and Great Northern railway (M&GN), which served the coast up to the 1890s; he told me that it is known by railway historians as the 'Midland Going Nowhere'. The fascination of the lines around here is evident in a newsletter of the M&GN Circle, in which I read an explanation of why the line at the Mundesley branch was closed back in 1893. In the newsletter, Mike Back explains that a letter from some parliamentary agents to the Board of Trade provides the answer: 'The letter states that the proposed branch had not been constructed by the E&MR [East and Midland Railway] because the "pecuniary results of that company did not justify further expenditure".' If only they had waited: the day-trippers and holidaymakers were soon to arrive.

They had certainly arrived on the day of my visit: the car park was double-racked, the buffet room was packed and the platform lined with folks ready to take their snapshots. There was something beautifully idyllic about the whole atmosphere and I understood the appeal of railway history. But there is more than that at Weybourne because there are also military vehicles a little way down the road, at another heritage centre, and as this East Anglian coast was the front line of the defence of our island against Nazi Germany, this is an important element of modern history.

But above all, Weybourne has the charm of its mill, its church and the strange wildness of that shingle beach.

Sheringham

In the report of the Royal Commission of 1911, the author understood what process of erosion was occurring here:

At Skelding Hill, just west of Sheringham, the cliff is much higher and landslips become an important consideration; but as the foreshore is still solid chalk, the seaward creep of the whole hill need not be taken into account. If the sea-defences of Sheringham last, in a few years the seaward face of this hill also will become sloped back, as there is no connected mass of high ground to yield much water. Along this part of the Norfolk coast I think that much of the land drainage escapes through fissures in the chalk, as springs given out under the sea, and thus the springs do not cause land-slips.

This describes the characteristic cliff feature now: an incline, in the lower cliffs, around 45 degrees back, with deep cuts into the chalk forming a succession of v-shaped cliff fronts.

The same author, who obviously visited all the places he wrote about, gave a very close-up account of Sheringham's efforts a century ago to preserve its seafront:

When the first groyne was put up the immediate result was a greatly increased rate of erosion on the lee side and under Beeston Hill. The travel of the beach was stopped by the groyne ... the foreshore to the east showed only bare chalk, and a constant succession of land-slips fell from Beeston Hill.

Today, the groynes there are reinforced by supporting strong high-density timber, and this is needed constantly, as although the modern groyne looks and feels as solid as steel, it is still ravaged and damaged by the waves' power.

The same author, continuing his report in 1911, was deeply interested in the problems at Beeston (later Beeston Regis). He fastened on to the topic of the flints – flint being the one hard older rock in this area. He saw then the importance of this for the making of defences:

The question arises: what is the life of a flint-pebble when exposed to sea-action? This is a most important point to settle, for the parts of our eastern and southern coast which are eroded most rapidly depend for their protection on a beach mainly composed of flint pebbles.

He studied the flints and concluded that if some strategy could be created in which they could be used in defence, it would work better than any other available material.

Today, Sheringham is a leisurely place with an atmosphere of relaxation – a place where people stroll and loiter, eat well and stare at the sea. The pier and the Little Theatre cater for the cultural side it definitely encourages, and there is still the impressive Hotel de Paris overlooking the pier landing, the hotel being once a haunt of the rich and famous, notably Oscar Wilde.

The sea defences are at the centre, as opposed to the south, which reaches to Beeston Regis and then Overstrand, or the north, which has the usual crumbling cliffs that edge Upper Sheringham, where the golf club borders the dunes.

I talked to a fisherman here, on a sunny day in September – a true St Michael's summer – and as I sat and watched the sea birds scanning the waves, a boat caught my eye, down on the pebbles below, near the landing, and a man nearby saw my inspection of it.

'It's my boat,' he said, his Norfolk accent making the last word boot. He was in the blue garb of the seaman and his face was weathered and tanned; his fair hair was ponytailed and he was lithe, athletic, fit enough to push that boat out if he only had a puddle beneath it. He was crabbing in between work on the distant wind farm, which could be seen that day, 8 miles out to sea. The water that day was peaceful as a full washing-up bowl, but of course, that was not always so.

I asked about the fishing for crabs and lobsters and he explained that today only six boats worked from Sheringham, and that young men wanting to learn the craft would have to spend about £20,000 on the boat and the kit. They would also have to go out with someone like him to learn the skills in the first place. We talked about the contrast between trawling (which never happens around there now) and the old ways of selecting keeps and throwaways from the crab pots. Plenty of what a man found there would be thrown back, he told me. He worked at sea from March to October, and caught an immense amount of the harvest of the sea, using ten pots each trip out.

Talk moved on to erosion, and he spoke about the abandonment of the coast down south, around Happisburgh and places like Bacton. He lamented the attitude of the authorities, who were applying notions of controlled loss. This was all very well for the long term, but the poor folk living on the edge had no future, he thought. He was a good advert for life at Sheringham, living healthily and in the open air; he wouldn't swap it for anything. What about the dangers of the sea? He explained that the wind farm off Weybourne and Cley was fixed on a sand bank, and although it took a long time to establish, it was sound. He added that the water we were looking at was shallow, about 25 metres deep on the whole, so given reasonable weather, it was a safe place to work.

In contrast, if we look at the old days, when the fishing really dominated the area, the seafront café where people sit today to stare at the sea was once an important location in the whelking industry. The house was called 'Whelk Copper', and oral history testifies that it was once a hive of production. Peter Brooks, in his booklet on the town, writes, 'Local people recall the thick black smoke that used to pour from the copper chimneys on its western end.'

In earlier times, before Sheringham itself developed, Upper Sheringham Hythe was the spot where the fishermen worked and went to sea. In the Middle Ages there were fish retailers and boat builders, and by the end of the sixteenth century there was a record of seventeen boats at work, with another five working part-time. Of course, before its status as largely a holiday destination, Sheringham had vessels of considerable sizes working there, such as the luggers, seen throughout Victorian times. These had a large crew and went out for herring and mackerel as well as crabs.

As usual with any tale of East Anglian ports, maintenance of the harbour and front were a problem. Over a long period prior to the late Tudor years, there was extensive neglect, so that in 1583, following a plea for help, a plan for a harbour was issued. Work was finished by 1585, with the use of solid oak timber and stone. But, as local historian Peter Brooks sums up, 'The harbour did not survive for any length of time.' That is a familiar story.

Sheringham grew steadily, from a population of just 392 in 1801, to 1,134 in 1841. The directories, as is so often the case, provide useful figures: *White's Directory*, in 1836 records 'curing houses, twenty-six herring boats and a number of small fishing boats'. The close neighbour, Beeston Regis, had almost 200 people by the mid-Victorian years, and that added to the general prosperity. The other influential directory, Kelly's, notes, in 1875, that Sheringham then had 200 boats. The final stamp of approval stating that the town had arrived in some kind of modernity was the railway, and the connection was made in 1906 to the Great Eastern network, which worked from King's Cross.

With prosperity came the need to fight the sea, or at least to keep the waves at bay. My continuing chronicle of destruction by the various forces of erosion applies here too, with some severity. Records again show a steady stream of victims, such as the end of the Crown Inn in 1800, and if some idea of lost land is needed, Peter Brooks informs us that an enclosure map of 1811 'shows a considerable amount of land to the seaward of the Two Lifeboats Coffee House' (that is, to the south). One of the most telling details from social history of the results of the sea's destruction comes from this town, because it had a recreation patch of land known as The Green, and events there included a fair. All this was destroyed. As will be seen later with my account of Southwold, the habit of putting cottages and sheds on the beach was an invitation to attack, and indeed in 1877, several such buildings were flooded and taken.

Peter Brooks notes that the Urban District Council in the early twentieth century spent £1,800 a year on sea defences. Since then, all the usual strategies have been in place, from groynes to rock revetments.

Cromer and Shipden

In my own quest to know Norfolk, I have to celebrate the 'island' of the Cromer Ridge. If one travels from Hunstanton along the coast to the other side of Cromer, at Overstrand, perhaps, the arrival of the wooded and farmed stretch from the south of Weybourne to Cromer is noticeable by contrast. The marshes and flats then lie just behind, and as you enter Upper Sheringham, then Sheringham itself, the Runtons and Beeston Regis, the feeling is that this is a separate place in some ways, not quite so raw and exposed. In Upper Sheringham it is plain that there is a vista of green fields, woods and farms, with the line of the sea beyond; the view could be a bright, gaudy Ravilious print, with the lines of high walls and flint-sided homes between the National Trust land and the fringes of Sheringham itself, with the newish builds and its school, golf club and businesses.

One very plain loss from Cromer was the first lighthouse, which had been constructed in 1719. On the map made by Milne referred to in the last chapter, the lighthouse is shown at the cliff edge; thirty years later, it was very much threatened, and in 1866 it was washed away.

Writing sixty years ago, Arthur Mee began his account of Cromer with an essential piece of information for anyone wishing to acquaint themselves with that lovely town's history:

> If we would go back to its beginning we must tell the story of the forest bed of the Pliocene Age before men walked the earth, for its fossil trees are still exposed when the fierce storms rage across the grey North Sea. Here on these noble cliffs stands Cromer, a new Cromer we must call it, for an older one lies down beneath the waves, and this is a Cromer which has defied the sea with a strong wall and put the church and houses beyond its reach.

In the great Domesday survey, completed in 1086, Cromer was merely a part of a place called Shipden, as noted in my introduction, and through the medieval years, land owned at Shipden was recorded, with names such as Godric, Halmod de Bidon and Sir Nicholas de Weyland being mentioned. In Domesday, Shipden was listed, and had two areas: Shipden juxta Mare and Shipden juxta Felbrigg, the latter being where Cromer is now. Shipden started to be labelled 'Crowe-mere' and then Cromer. Later still, in the sixteenth and seventeenth centuries it came into the ownership of the famous Paston family, well known in literature for the letters they produced. But as a directory of the late nineteenth century records:

> In 1611 Sir William Paston was lord of the manor, called Wayland's in Cromer, and was held of the Duchy of Lancaster, and it is said that great parts of the land belonging to it were swallowed up by the sea.

Maps produced over the centuries have logged the gradual loss of land. John Speed's map of 1610 shows land that has been lost; places around Cromer that have gone are Shipden, Foulness and Clare. Foulness was on a headland near Overstrand, and even had a lighthouse. Three hundred years ago, Foulness was a place with a name and some kind of identity.

As for Shipden, it was about a third of a mile from the pier at Cromer. It is most unsettling to recall that Shipden once had two churches; the village was important enough to be listed in Domesday, when it seems that over a hundred people lived there. In 1086, the lord was Bishop William of Thetford, and in 1285 there was the first mention of a market being held there. It was a reasonable size under the Conqueror, having seventeen households.

Of course, Shipden, being gone, has its oral tales and traditional legends. The outstanding one was of the steamer as told in my introduction, in which the boat struck something known to local fishermen as Church Rock, the remains of a 54-foot tower.

As for Cromer itself, the author of the 1911 report of the Royal Commission summed up the measures taken then:

> At Cromer the sea defences have been constructed under Acts of Parliament passed in 1845 and 1899, the former of which constituted a body called the Cromer Protection Commissioners, and entrusted them with the duty of protecting the town. The Act of 1899 extended the powers of the Commissioners. A sea wall was built under the powers given by the Act of 1845 and additions were made to it under the Act of 1899, while timber groynes have been constructed to hold up the beach in front of the wall. The cost of these protective works, including that of a promenade and approaches, has been over £34,000.
>
> [The figure quoted needs to be multiplied by around 60 for a modern equivalent sum.]

'Poppy Land', Sidestrand and Overstrand

It takes something extraordinary for a little coastal hamlet to be noticed, but that is what happened here. One visitor transformed this little range of coast into almost a dream. It was his own dreamlike idyll, but he succeeded in making it virtually a shrine.

Writers and artists have often made areas of Britain into places of pilgrimage: examples include Wordsworth's Dove Cottage in Grasmere and Thomas Hardy's Dorchester. Norfolk certainly has comparable locations, and this spot is one of them – made immensely popular by a London literary man.

Clement Scott (1841–1904) was a drama critic, working mainly for *The Daily Telegraph*. He also wrote his own works, covering travel writing, essays and plays. The portrait of him in *Theatre* magazine, when he was about forty, shows a solid, sturdy man with a full moustache, scholarly glasses and a forthright expression on his face over some determinedly folded arms. He was born in Hoxton, London, and was educated at Marlborough College. Before he made his name as a writer he was a civil servant at the War Office. He was only twenty-two when he started writing for *The Sunday Times* and other magazines, including Thomas Hood's more light-hearted journal, *Fun*.

Scott would have been remembered in the footnotes of theatre and literary history as the drama critic who made the mistake of saying things in an interview that cost him his position in journalism, had it not been for his visit to the Norfolk coast. Yes, he moved in high circles: he was a friend and associate of most of the influential dramatists of his day. But it was a feature article he wrote, printed in *The Telegraph* in 1883, that created a stir and indeed brought rich and influential people of the time to Sidestrand, Overstrand and Cromer.

One of the most emotional and significant tales associated with the crumbling cliffs of Norfolk arose from this feature, called 'Poppy Land', which later expanded into a series of pieces and then was printed as a book, *Poppy Land: Papers Descriptive of Scenery on the East Coast*, in 1886. Scott makes a point of insisting that England has its own wonderful beauty, as good as anywhere in Europe that was at the time attracting more and more Brits – especially Germany and Switzerland. Then he describes his encounter with his Norfolk idyll:

It was on one of the most beautiful days of the lovely month of August, a summer morning with a cloudless blue sky overhead and a sea without a ripple washing on the yellow sands, that I turned my back on perhaps the prettiest watering-place of the east coast and walked along the cliffs to get a blow and a look at the harvest that had just begun. It was the old story. At a mile removed from the seaside town I had left I did not find a human being.

Scott's articles and book were to make Overstrand and Sidestrand very popular holiday destinations – exactly the kind of outcome he would have hated, as the point of his writing was to stress the tranquillity of the area. As Neil Storey pointed out: 'The spiritual heart of Poppy Land was the ruined tower of Sidestrand Church', which was precariously near the cliff edge when he was writing. A celebrated photograph taken around 1900 of this shows a party of visitors sitting with their dog on the clifftop, with the tower behind them, and a young woman by the side of the tower, peeping over the precarious edge.

Scott wrote:

> So serious has been the cliff fall eastward and westward from Cromer that the frightened villagers of our little hamlet have moved their tiny church a quarter of a mile landward, and have left their old tower and their buried dead enclosed in a churchyard doomed to destruction but making its loneliness and melancholy one of the most pathetic and picturesque corners of the land.

The irony of his use of the beauty of the poppies in the poem he wrote at the opening of his book cannot have been lost on the readers a little later, in the Great War. His poem was called *The Garden of Sleep*, and it has these lines:

> *For a tower in ruins stands guard o'er the deep,*
> *At whose feet are green graves of dear women asleep!*
> *Did they love as I love, when they lived by the sea?*
> *Did they wait, as I wait, for the days that may be?*
> *Was it hope or fulfilling that entered each breast,*
> *Ere death gave release, and the poppies gave rest?*

The romantic tower finally tumbled into the waves in 1916.

As for his beloved Overstrand and Sidestrand, two communities side by side and the very core of Poppy Land, they benefitted from this notoriety, as people bought property there or stayed there in comfortable residences. Yet the list of losses to the sea goes on here too, as one hotel there plunged into the waters in the 1950s. But at Clifton Way there has been the trial of what is called riprap, a boulder brought from Norway, in addition to the usual standard methods of staying the destructive tides. Riprap is composed of a mixture of rocks, usually granite and limestone. The theory at the moment is that riprap may be moved by the sea, but some of the rocks used at Sheringham and Cromer are massive.

All this desire for solidity and permanence is at odds with what Lady Battersea wrote about on her life in Overstrand a century ago:

> Norfolk as a county always seems to me to be very self-sufficient, running away, as it were, into the great Northern Ocean. To a large extent the inhabitants have preserved their old habits, old customs, old manners of speech. ... The old cottages of the fisher folk in Overstrand are built of beautiful grey cobbles collected from the beach, the roofs of a dark red tile so that they are mostly of picturesque aspect.

Interestingly, as she was surrounded by the new fancy residences and hotels, she noted that the result of Scott's writings on Poppy Land was an influx of visitors that caused radical adjustments: 'For about ten weeks in the summer it would be difficult to find the owners of these houses at home in them ... the inhabitants live in strange little makeshift dwellings, even in railway carriages.'

Trimingham

In 2014, the owners of caravans on the cliffs at Trimingham requested permission to roll back their properties, as the cliffs were eroding, and were very near the park. This was given, and it seems that the sea is winning here. This is a place with high cliffs and great geological fascination in the chalk, which retains rich depths of material of interest to students of the pre-historical record. There has been a Coastguard station, and there were once ruins of an old beacon.

White's Directory of 1883 notes:

> Like Cromer, Trimingham is subject to the encroachments of the ocean, which washed away two farmhouses and several acres of land in

1822. A breakwater was erected in 1842 by the late Sir T.F. Buxton....
At present six breakwaters are in course of construction.

The same directory finds it right to mention one of the strangest legends in Norfolk: 'The church stands on the cliffs and is said to have been visited in the dark ages by many pilgrims who came to see the head of John the Baptist.'

We have a useful profile of the community in this same source, because the listing of inhabitants includes six farmers, a shopkeeper, a schoolmistress, a wheelwright, a carrier and a lime burner. The vicar was Abraham Matchett. In the mid-Victorian years, the Buxton family seems to have run the show, not only working hard against the destructive waves, but also paying for the building of the school in 1849.

Mundesley

Mundesley is always associated with the poet William Cowper, as he stayed there in 1795 with his cousin, mainly to help lift his depression. His stay was not always pleasant, though, because he notes, 'My walks on the sea shore have been paid for by swelled and inflamed eye-lids.' He was impressed by the terrain, but only for the worst of reasons: 'The cliff here is a height that is terrible to look down from ... but though to have been dashed to pieces would have been best for me, I shrunk from the precipice.'

As a county guide notes, 'Cowper's Mundesley was a quieter version of Cromer, visited by gentlefolk for its bathing and fresh air.' Back in the Domesday of 1086 it was 'Museleai' and had been given to William de Warenne by the Conqueror. A man called Grinkel owned 30 acres. Francis Blomefield, writing in 1808, notes that John Bradfield of Burnham Thorpe owned the place in the reign of James I.

By the nineteenth century it had not really grown much at all, having only 453 people there, according to a directory of the time. But in the 1840s, as a reflection of the peril along the coast, it was chosen as a Coastguard station. In the early twentieth century, the population increased to nearly 700, the railway, coming in 1898, having an influence on that growth.

Today, Mundesley, together with Overstrand and Trimingham, lacks funding in the fight against the sea. In the summary of the authority's plan for this area, we have: 'The new policy option for the majority of this length of coast is to no longer maintain existing timber groynes and revetments and to allow coastal retreat.' This is not unique: such decisions are being made in hundreds of coastal locations, and finance determines where investment goes.

Mundesley has, along with all the Norfolk coastal resorts, seen its share of storms, wrecks and terrible drowning. In 1858 there was a typical such incident when a Yarmouth vessel was stranded with the loss of all hands in a gale. In contrast, the loss of land was perhaps so common that it was less reported, but in the 1850s there were concerns, and even *The Times* pitched in with warnings and chastisements regarding the encroachments of the sea. In 1852, one report chose to focus on this part of Norfolk:

> The town of Cromer has been kept standing by well-sinking; so also have a single house and grounds in Mundesley. It seems to be quite forgotten that these fortifications, as the sea eats away on each side of them, will first become promontories, and then islands, unless the whole line of 20 miles is encased with stone-work.

In 1915, Mundesley, with its neighbours, was subject to national attention when the Zeppelin airships came across the Channel. *The Times* chose to tell its readers that Sandringham was under threat and that on 20 January, an airship went over Hunstanton and then passed directly over Sandringham. Readers were informed that the thing was like 'a large balloon, pointed at each end, and shaped like a sausage'. There was some doubt as to whether or not bombs had been dropped on Cromer, but eventually the rumour was denied. Still, worries over coastal erosion moved into the inside pages of the papers when it was reported: 'Some of the Mundesley fisher folk insist that they saw six of these huge aircraft, of which, soon after passing over Bacton, sailed south-west in the direction of Yarmouth.'

In more recent times, Mundesley has had drama enough as a result of cliff erosion. In September 1929, there was a cliff fall of massive proportions: 40,000 tons of earth fell on to the shore. The press reported: 'There is a large crack a little way from the new cliff edge and a further fall seems likely.' The owners of the lost land were Norman and had been given the land by William, who rewarded his followers in the invasion enterprise. Ironically, the field was for corn and had just been cut, and the height of the drama involved Mr Isaac Temple of Trunch, who was harrowing at the time. He told a reporter that he had just turned the harrow around from the edge, 'when he heard a noise like thunder' and ran for his life. His horse bolted and he found a safe place. He said that he saw 200 feet of land, freshly worked, disappear completely.

Just ten minutes before the fall, a couple had been sitting on the beach below. Some protecting angel was watching over them, we might think. A well-used footpath to the beach was destroyed, and overall, this was a warning, following an even more large-scale fall at Trimingham a year earlier, where 80,000 tons of earth was lost.

Between the summer of 1950 and the winter of 1954, Mundesley was the focus of real concern, when the church there was in danger of utter destruction. In May 1950, the Reverend Gedge at the church told his congregation that he intended to petition the King in order to find some help to save his church from erosion. The Venerable Perowne preached the sermon on that occasion and expressed support for the measure.

The church dated back to the 1300s and £3,000 had been spent on it in the first decade of the twentieth century. Before that, it had lain derelict for a very long time and had been described as no more than a heap of old masonry. In 1850 the church was 100 yards from the cliff edge, but in 1950 it was only a few feet away. In July 1949, geologist W.S. Mobbs told the church rector that there was a serious risk of disaster there, and suggested using a revetment and groynes.

Seven months after that announcement, there was a massive fall of earth from the cliff near to the church, resulting in only about 50 feet remaining from the edge of the churchyard to the edge of the cliff. The Reverend Gedge, whose earlier plea had clearly been ignored, told the press that more falls were likely before that winter. Then, in May 1953, there was open panic as no progress had been made in the matter.

From 1946 to 1953 – such a frighteningly short period – the church was 20 feet nearer the edge. The sea was 100 feet below, so any fall or slippage would have threatened complete annihilation. There was a parochial church meeting, and that attracted a reporter from *The Times*, who wrote:

> The rector stated the problem bluntly by asking the meeting, 'Is it wise to continue maintaining the church in its present superb state of preservation ... only to see it crumble into a pile of rubble ... or should we decide to neglect the repair of the present building and devote our energies to raising a fund to build a new church farther inland?'

The decision was to build a wall. A rock revetment had dealt with normal tides, but any abnormal tides would be a real threat, so a high sea wall was wanted. The catch was that the cost would have to be met by Erpingham rural district council, but the council engineers did not agree on the topic of the sea wall. The business came to an impasse, and the reporter ended with some rhetoric:

> Meanwhile, any visitor standing near the edge of the cliff with the rector and listening to his calm statement of the case cannot fail to be impressed with a sense of danger, whether it be in fact as near, or not quite so near, as the rector feels.

There was still some disagreement near the end of 1954, when there was a public inquiry into the matter, and there it was suggested by the Erpingham council that an enlargement of the existing revetment would be the best move. The Reverend Gedge was still not content.

Bacton

As one writer in the early nineteenth century summed up:

> Bacton has suffered much from the encroachment of the sea. In the description of lands appropriated to the priory of Broomholme are the names of many places which are now quite obsolete, the sites on which they stood now being occupied by the ocean.

This defines exactly what the fascination with these lost places is. Even at the time when that statement was written, when George IV was regent, writers and students of the terrain here were fully aware that the old maps now showed places that were no more, and there was a demand for guesswork and conjecture.

The same writer did at least monitor some of the nearby land, such as Witton Hall, the seat of Lord Wodehouse, which had been built by John Norris in 1770, and there was Paston Hall, owned by a certain John Mack in 1820. But details of the lost land and its dwellers were sparse even then. We do know that there was also Keswic, close to Bacton, and in the old courts rolls we have lumped together 'Bacton cum Broomhole and Keswic'. The same writer on Bacton notes of Keswic:

> Time has so effectively cast his mantle over this once rising hamlet that but little can be gathered as to it former extent, population or importance. Its situation was to the east of Bacton, and was generally called Keswic or Casewic, and appears to have been part of the manor of Bacton.

In 1382 there was a church at Keswic, dedicated to St Clement. The account by Blomefield continues to explain that there is no record of when it was ruined, but he adds, 'The churchyard is now a garden, in the occupation of Mr Francis Marshall. ... The road to the beach is also cut through part of it ... many cart-loads of bones were removed.'

In the 1911 Royal Commission, the report author was deeply concerned about Bacton and the stretch of coast down to Yarmouth. His recommendation was to focus on the dunes and his summary of events over the previous half-century give us a very striking picture of the losses:

> This stretch of coast consists, for the most part, of low-lying sands which are difficult to protect against the sea. There has, however, been no serious erosion in recent years. On parts of this stretch the sand dunes have moved inland; for example in 1839 the ruined tower of Eccles church was half buried in the sand-hills; in 1862 the dunes had moved so far inland that the tower was seaward of them, and in

1895 the tower was destroyed by the waves. In view of the fact that an encroachment of the sea upon this stretch of coast would damage wide areas of low-lying land, it is necessary that the natural defences – the sand dunes – should be most carefully fostered and maintained.

This Royal Commission was partly written by men who had actually walked on the coasts they wrote about; I will be quoting this document throughout, as the comments and insights are by those who were familiar with the terrain. Often their comments begin with 'The last time I walked this 2-mile track ...'

Happisburgh

For visitors to Norfolk, the first point about this village is that it is pronounced 'haze-bro' and that would catch out the supposed German spies who were feared to have landed around this coast in the Second World War, along with other tough differences between spelling and sounding such as Slough or Slaithwaite. Indeed, from time to time the papers report these kinds of difficulties for visitors to Norfolk. In 1991, John Fairbairn wrote to *The Times* on the subject and quoted Happisburgh, along with Stiffkey (pronounced *Stooky)* and Mundesley, which becomes 'Munsley'.

This is a special place for anyone studying the former inhabitants – from however long ago – of this coast. This is because archaeology has found a substantial series of artefacts that present astounding evidence of the place from about 800,000 years ago: most amazingly, ancient human footprints. These have been located as well as such items as mammoth bones. The humans who walked here have been labelled Homo antecessor. The footprints are there alongside the groynes. They give evidence of this version of mankind, sometimes called 'Pioneer man', who has also been studied at Atapuerca in Northern Spain. An analysis of the Norfolk prints has shown that they were made by six or seven people, walking south. One report, in *The Independent*, explains, 'It is likely that these people were foraging for shellfish, edible tubers or seaweed in a prehistoric landscape inhabited by deer, mammoth, rhino, horse, giant elk, hyena and possibly a sabre-toothed cat.'

The prints were most likely made by a family group, who were short in stature, probably from 3 to 5½ feet tall. *The Independent* feature contains a remark by Professor Chris Stringer that places these people in context; he told the writer, Steve Connor, that they may have been the first of perhaps nine separate colonisations of Britain over the past million years.

In early 2015, the village featured in a news feature with a story so often repeated: 'A bungalow is balanced on a cliff edge. The house next door is already gone. All that's left is the back garden, where the displaced owner lives in a caravan.' The accompanying picture shows a cluster of small homes above a crumbling cliff, with planks of wood and window frames down on the sand below. This is now a sadly familiar image. The feature adds that the medieval church and manor house will be gone. As usual, timber revetments had been in position but had disintegrated. Sea defences were built here in the 1950s. Today, as is always the case, the remedy is in spending money on the defences.

Seven years before this, there had been a startling proposal put forward by Natural England. The Happisburgh village website reported then that such a plan was a confirmation of defeat:

> The move would also see a millennium of history vanish under the sea. The village of Hickling is typical of what would be lost. It is mentioned in Domesday Book under the name Hikelinga and a priory was founded there in 1185.... The village has been flooded many times before, including in 1287, when 180 people lost their lives.

The sea has definitely wreaked destruction around Happisburgh: the sands and the gales have played their lethal part in the wrecking of so many vessels. In December 1770, for instance, HMS *Peggy* was driven ashore and thirty-two crewmen were buried in the churchyard. Again, in 1807, HMS *Hunter* came to grief here and the crew were lost.

The Council for the Preservation of Rural England began to play some part in the attempts to protect the coast as far back as the 1930s. In 1936, area committees were formed, with a chairman. They met in Beccles initially, and speeches were made, with a local correspondent commenting, 'They had a very wonderful coastline from Yarmouth to Happisburgh to look after.' He was obviously thinking of the fact that lost land at Happisburgh was always reported, usually with a sense of drama and sensation. Looking back, this only seems to be a typical instance of a right move being made, but with no immediate funding.

Twenty years later, people were still making plans to try to do something about the crumbling cliffs, and in the aftermath of the horrendous 1953 floods, a sea wall was planned by the Smallburgh Rural District Council. The council met at Stalham and submitted a request for a sub-committee to work on a second line of defence of some low sand hills. These had been severely damaged in the 1953 floods. The focus of the work was to be at Cart Gap, Happisburgh, extending 8 miles south at Winterton. Suggestions were that the wall should be at least 18 feet high in some parts. There was a degree of optimism in this thinking, as the people involved argued that there would be no maintenance required; they were confident that there would be no 'tidal scour'.

But time went on, and although some work was done in more recent times, notably in 1986, money has been placed for sea defences at this stretch of coast. In the 1980s, the Anglian Water Authority was leading the campaign for such investment. One report at the time said that £15 million a year would be needed over ten years to help East Anglia where, as the authority argued, there was 'serious risk of a repeat of the 1953 floods', and they located the 'danger spots' on the Happisburgh to Winterton coastline.

In more recent years, other places in specific danger have been identified, such as the Cliff House guest house, whose owners were waiting to see how far the 2006 winter storms had 'nibbled at the cliff before deciding to re-open', according to the press. A report explained that Diana Wrightson and Jill Morris had run the house for the previous eleven years. Diana said, 'Every year it becomes more and more difficult to decide.' They moved out, finally, and with great reluctance.

The Independent spoke to Diana and Jill in 2008, and they were joined by other locals, such as Trevor Beeby, who said, when asked about the safety of his home, 'It's always in your mind, from when you get up until you go to bed. ... No one will do anything for us. We just have to make the best of it.' One stunning fact was uncovered by the author of the feature, Michael Savage. He met two people who wanted to use their Beach Road bungalow for collateral for a loan. Expecting a valuation of £80,000, they were told that the bank's value for it was £1 – because of chronic coastal erosion. Savage noted that, when the place is no more, there will be 'no fewer than eighteen listed buildings, including its Grade I listed church, built in the thirteenth century', that go with it.'

But the most compelling story of modern Happisburgh relates to Peter Boggis, whom we shall meet again in Suffolk.

The report of the 1911 Royal Commission tackled the problems of the stretch of coast from Happisburgh to Yarmouth by giving most attention to the need for the Commissioners of Sewers to play their part in helping to preserve the dunes. The authors pointed out that, back at the time of the Norman Conquest, there was one great estuary in the area, but that later, this was blocked up. The Commission of Sewers was responsible for this place, and reported the testimony from a Mr Horner regarding the dunes. Horner's views were included in the report:

> Mr Horner ... stated that, where the grass was exposed to the keen east winds it was exceedingly difficult to get it to grow, and that where it thrives, it is generally sheltered by some little knoll. The Commission rely almost entirely on the width of the sand hills, which is generally from 25 to 30 feet, to withstand any great storm, with the exception that, if a bad breach occurs which should be dealt with immediately, herring swills are obtained and filled with stones lashed together, and put tier on tier, the sand being allowed to accumulate over them.

Astoundingly, the Commissioners back then had their own prototype of the modern gabion: the concept of stones gathered into a netted container, i.e. swills, which are framed withy baskets.

In an optimistic effort, Malcolm Kirby has led a movement to preserve the place with a strategy that admits that the sea will always win the battle along the present coastline, so preserving the village means moving it back. With financial help and community co-operation, his solution is working. After the awful experience of having twenty-seven houses lost in thirty years, now the community is fighting back.

Fishermen's boats on a typical landing at Cromer, with the RNLI Henry Blogg Museum in the background, named after the 'greatest lifeboatman of all time'.

Crab pots at Sheringham – relics from a declining trade.

A clear view of the pier and coastline at Cromer in 1912. (Author's collection)

The cliffs at Cromer.

This image of old Cromer shows the hotels built in the boom years. (Author's collection)

Dunes on The Wash coast.

The model of old Dunwich created at the museum there. (Jane Hamilton, Dunwich Museum)

An old image of a Dunwich ship. (*Suffolk Sea-Borders*, H. Alker Tripp, 1926)

A view of Gorleston Pier in the early twentieth century, where fishermen and visitors could take shelter in the 'cosies'.

ROUGH SEA OFF GORLESTON.

A postcard showing rough seas attacking Gorleston Pier.

The Children's Corner at Gorlestone-on-Sea. This was recently battered and needed repairs.

Writers Edward Clodd (left) and Thomas Hardy at Aldeburgh. (*Memoirs of a Bookman*, James Milne)

This is the view of the Hotel de Paris that Oscar Wilde would have seen while staying in Cromer.

The famous Hotel de Paris in Cromer today.

Hunstanton beach today.

This old postcard shows the banded, 'candy' cliffs at Hunstanton.

A rare snap of local history: tents on Hunstanton beach back in the 1950s.

A 1950s postcard showing the swing bridge at Lowestoft.

The blown sluice at the Marshland Drain. (*The Illustrated London News*, October 1862)

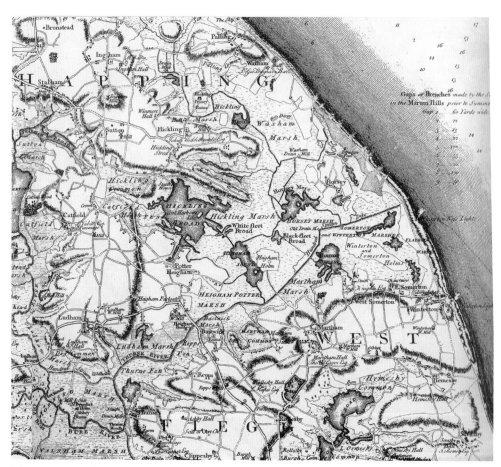

The coast around Palling and Waxham, 1797. (The Milne map, Hull University)

Some of the ancient tree stumps that have emerged from the sea near Cromer Pier.

A True and Perfect

RELATION

OF

The great Damages done by the late
Great Tempeſt, and overflowing

OF THE

TYDE

Upon the Coaſts of

𝕷𝖎𝖓𝖈𝖔𝖑𝖓𝖘𝖍𝖎𝖗𝖊 and County of 𝕹𝖔𝖗𝖋𝖔𝖑𝖐.

ALSO

An accompt of the Ships caſt away, Houſes beaten
down, and Men, Women and Children drowned by
the late Inundation.

𝕸𝖎𝖙𝖍 𝕬𝖑𝖑𝖔𝖜𝖆𝖓𝖈𝖊.

LONDON,
Printed in the Year, 1671.

The title page of an early tract on floods and tides. (Hull University)

The ruined, ivy-covered church at Poppy Land. (*Poppy Land*, 1886)

The heart of Clement Scott's Poppy Land idyll in Norfolk. (*Poppy Land*, 1886)

One of the many beautiful posters that promoted tourism via Britain's railways.

A typical coastal scene of reeds and groynes.

The title page of the 1911 Royal Commission report.

ROYAL COMMISSION ON COAST EROSION
AND AFFORESTATION.

VOLUME III.
(PART I.)

THIRD (AND FINAL) REPORT

OF THE

ROYAL COMMISSION

Appointed to inquire into and to report on certain Questions affecting

COAST EROSION,

THE RECLAMATION OF TIDAL LANDS, AND AFFORESTATION

IN THE

UNITED KINGDOM.

Presented to both Houses of Parliament by Command of His Majesty.

LONDON:
PUBLISHED BY HIS MAJESTY'S STATIONERY OFFICE.
To be purchased, either directly or through any Bookseller, from
WYMAN AND SONS, LIMITED, FETTER LANE, E.C., and 32, ABINGDON STREET, S.W.; or
OLIVER & BOYD, TWEEDDALE COURT, EDINBURGH; or
E. PONSONBY, LTD., 116, GRAFTON STREET, DUBLIN.

PRINTED BY
WYMAN AND SONS, LIMITED, 109, FETTER LANE, E.C.

1911.

[Cd. 5708.]   Price 3s.

Floods in the Fens – the Syphon Dam in the 1862 floods. (*The Illustrated London News*)

A very clear view of a cliff being undercut by the tide.

A Yarmouth boat on the raised beach.

A postcard featuring the great days of Yarmouth holidays: the scenic railway and donkey rides.

An old image of the old tower and yacht station at Great Yarmouth.

Note: All photographs by the author, unless otherwise stated.

Eccles next the Sea

This is the classic instance of a coastal settlement site being lost and buried under the sand. This probably happened around 1570, and from time to time ruins are exposed to the air. Together with some excavations, knowledge of the place has gradually been gained. As is often the case, aerial photographs have highlighted the remains more effectively.

In 1908, some stone circles were found there, and inside circles of wood there were others made from wattle. Archaeological digs have uncovered remains of sheep and pig bones there too. A report by the Norfolk Heritage Explorer notes: 'The exposed remains of a series of wells, a roadway and the walls of St Mary's churchyard and scattered tower fragments are visible on aerial photographs.' But even after the 1953 floods, the report adds, the stone remains of some kind of structure 'were not clear enough for a definite identification and therefore it is not possible to deduce whether it is part of a medieval settlement site.'

Over the years, there have been sightings of various ruins, such as in this report in 1947:

Part of the ruins of an ancient church, a burial ground with human skeletons and fragments of pottery has been uncovered by wind and waves at Eccles ... the church was eventually buried by sand ... the old tower remained standing until the great gale on 23 January 1895.

The records give evidence of a complete village there; repeated storms took their toll, notably in 1570 and 1604. After the latter storm, the people petitioned for a tax reduction, and at that date, as Guy Fawkes was trying to blow up Parliament, in Eccles there were just fourteen houses and 300 acres of land remaining. In 1845, *White's Directory* reported that it had then just fifty-three inhabitants and 253 acres of land 'divided into three farms, occupied by Cornelius Croxton, George Empson and Robert Thompson'. The state of the place at that time is emphasised by this comment in the same directory:

Eccles church [St Mary] ... is still standing, but is embedded to the height of the former walls of the church, in the accumulated sand hills which have been thrown up by the sea, and serve as a barrier against the too rapid encroachments of the tides.

Forty years later, in an updated *White's Directory*, Eccles is linked to Hempstead, the two places having been joined for reasons relating to the Poor Law. Hempstead had '9 acres, let for £12 and was awarded an enclosure. The poor have also the interest of £32 and a yearly rent of 3s 4d left by Mr A.C. Grey.'

By 1881, Eccles' population had dwindled to seventeen inhabitants. The 1883 *White's* gives figures of '253 acres' worked by 'John Clements and Jeremiah Whittaker'. The continuing fascination with that vulnerable church tower went on, with the remark that another storm – in 1862 – had swept away most of the old walls.

In 2012, the *Eastern Daily Press* printed a feature on Eccles, looking at 'the fleeting glimpse of Eccles' past' laid bare by the emergence of the old masonry again. The writer, Chris Hill, met a couple called Stannard, who are founder members of the Eccles Lost Village Project. Mr Stannard commented, regarding the now visible St Andrew's church foundations:

> We never knew when it was going to happen. If you spent time ringing people to get them to come along, by the time they arrived the tide would have come in and it would all be gone. … All we could do was plot it, photograph it and collect it.

The people of the Village Project staged an exhibition, the proceeds of which went towards the appeal to raise money for St Andrew's church. As well as the pictures, there are plenty of artefacts being gathered, but as Chris Hill pointed out, 'For a coastal dweller with a penchant for archaeology, the hungry ocean remains a double-edged sword – causing heartbreak by sweeping clifftop homes into the sea at Happisburgh, while revealing priceless historical artefacts a few miles away at Eccles-on-Sea.'

Sea Palling and Waxham

Sea Palling, which is a civil parish containing Waxham, derives its name from the Old English *Paelli ingas*, the settlement of Paelli's people. In 1841 there were 425 people there (in both places) and a century later, there were 478. Not much change there, it seems, but its history is far from constant. In Domesday, Palling was a place with nine villagers and fourteen smallholders, with 20 acres of meadows. There has been drama, though – the drama provided by the waves.

Waxham Parva has completely gone, including within its land some parts of the estate of Gelham Hall. The remains of the hall itself, which was a moated manor owned by St Benet's Abbey in the Early Norman Conquest period, now constitute large ditches, overgrown with trees. It appears that some earthworks there originally were part of a medieval fishpond. The Gelhams owned the estate until it was bought by Sir Thomas Wodehouse in 1521.

As to the progress and victory of the sea over Waxham, we have an account written by a monk who was at St Benet's Abbey, one John of Oxendes, who wrote this of the storm in 1287:

> the sea, agitated by the violence of the wind, burst through its accustomed limits, occupying towns, fields and other places adjacent to the coast ... it suffocated or drowned men and women sleeping in their beds, with infants in their cradles and it tore up houses from their foundations, with all they contained, and threw them into the sea with irrevocable damage.

Palling was seriously breached again in 1607. In 1655, and again in 1741, Waxham suffered extreme inundation. There was an attempt by Sir Berney Brograve (1726–97), a colourful character in Norfolk's history, to apply an old Act of Parliament to have work done on his flooded estate. His father had bought the estate in 1733, owning the manors of Waxham and Horsey, and their seat was initially at Waxham Hall. They built the Brograve Mill at Waxham to work as part of the drainage scheme there. In 1761, Sir Berney married Jane Hawker of Great Baddow in Essex, and after her death he got married again, to Jane Halcott of Litcham, with whom he had eleven children. The Brograves moved to Worstead House but still sometimes spent time at Waxham. Sir Berney became a notorious eccentric. One later writer said that 'he farmed his own land and had about a hundred workmen lodging in his house; these all dined in the great hall together, and Sir Berney every now and then "knocked down" a bullock for them to live upon.'

Clearly, he had a battle with the sea. But there was more to his eventful life than being a man ruined by the woes consequent on the encroachment of the German Ocean. Cheryl Nicol, a descendant of Sir Berney, has written his biography. She told the press, 'When I first started researching, nearly everything I found out was bad. He was a black-hearted man whose soul belonged to the devil. A reputation like that doesn't come free.' She told an interviewer that 'the North Sea swallowed his estates' and then, with the real heart of this emotional story looming almost like a scene from a Thomas Hardy novel, she added, 'The pattern of death matches the most severe flooding. As floodwater lay stagnant across the marshes, mosquitoes bred and spread deadly malaria, then known as fen ague.' Cheryl pointed out that 'In two days in 1793, he lost his second wife and their 18-year-old son.'

Legends and ghost stories grew around Sir Berney, and perhaps the tales of the paranormal have taken over from the factual details of his tough life. Unfortunately, Sir Berney's efforts to fight the floods failed, and there was nothing done to protect the place until more recent times. In the infamous 1953 floods, there were seven deaths here.

Of course, along with the terrors of the advancing sea come opportunities, just as war brings employment to some and death to others. In the case of Palling, the success was in smuggling, mostly such expensive and desirable commodities as tea and gin. As with other East Anglian coastal towns, crime and wrecks brought coastguards, and the Coastguard organisation came early to Palling, in 1822. Hand in hand with this came the lifeboat, and the first lifeboat station was in place by 1840.

Winterton-on-Sea

What has always struck travellers around Winterton has been the lighthouse and the 'very dangerous headland' at Winterton Ness, as one Victorian visitor put it. In the Domesday Book it is 'Wintretuna'. Defoe noted the dangerous area for ships off this location, and its lighthouse has been essential to shipping through the years. *White's Directory* of 1836 sums up the area: 'well known to the mariner as the most fatal headland between Scotland and London.'

Its notable land feature is the area known now as 'The Dunes'. In the late eighteenth century, marram grass was planted extensively to retain sand, and a large dune barrier developed, making a valley. Before that, as the 1836 directory stated:

> In 1665, by the sea encroaching on the cliffs, several large bones were found ... on 27 December a high tide caused such alarming sea-breaches at Winterton, Horsey and Waxham as to threaten destruction to all the level of marshes from thence to Yarmouth.

Once again, the listings in the directories give a useful guide to population: in 1836 there were six mariners, a lighthouse keeper, and Lieutenant Thomas RN, who was the officer of the coastguard.

A century before, when Defoe was in that area, he saw the very poor, makeshift nature of the fisher folk and farmers:

> As I went by land from Yarmouth northward along the shore towards Cromer ... I was surprised to see in all the way from Winterton, that the farmers had, and country people ... scarce a barn or a shed or a stable; nay, not the pales of their yards and gardens, not a hogsty, not a necessary-house, but what was built of old planks, beams, wales and timbers and the wrecks of ships, and ruins of mariners' and merchants' fortunes.

Hemsby

In terms of the most ancient history of the county, Hemsby was in the hundred of West Flegg, and is just 7 miles from Yarmouth. In the late nineteenth century there was land extending to 1,743 acres there. Hemsby was founded during the era of the Viking invasions; in Domesday it was recorded as 'Hamiesbei' and the entry is: 'a hamlet covering 43 meadow acres with fifty households, three slaves, two salt pans [flat expanses of salty land, with a mixture of minerals] and 160 sheep.'

Today, the sand dunes are subject to erosion and a campaign is running to save the beach at Hemsby. In contrast, 200 years ago, there was a National School, six farmers, gardeners, wheelwrights, millers and blacksmiths there, with the Blue Bell pub and Henry Gunn running the village store. In 1845, there was a population of 608. However modest the income of the place, back in Henry II's time, the King bothered to take what he could: 'homage of tenants, and two palfreys to have a market'. Edward I wanted ownership of 'wreck at sea, view of frankpledge, assize, free-warren, pillory and tumbrel'. Most of those words would have put the fear of God into the hearts of the locals. 'Frankpledge' was a system that formed groups of working men – tithings – and each man had to stand security for his peers. The other things were related to control (and profit from) crime. The 'tumbrel' was related to punishment, as it was a cart that tipped its load backwards, and was used to drag an offender around a parish, being a method of humiliation, like the stocks and pillory.

Caister-on-Sea

Caister was a Roman settlement, and together with Burgh Castle, it guarded the coast around the southern extent of the county. The position of the fort in Roman times was 3 kilometres further from the sea, and is located on the Bure estuary, with Burgh Castle opposite, closer to where the river Yare comes to join the southern part of the estuary. Consequently, in Roman times, the fort was placed on a small island; now there is land around the area where the excavations took place.

The fort was one of a line of installations along what was called the 'Saxon Shore' – with Brancaster up at The Wash and Burgh to the south. It was built around AD 200 and had a military strength of somewhere hear 1,000 men. The Roman name for one of the two forts (which one seems to be uncertain) was Gariannonum.

In the last few years, Caister has provided one of the most dramatic cases of a dwelling lost to the sea; in March 2013, a severe storm exposed some ruins. The *Eastern Daily Press* reported: 'Winds howled across the Norfolk beach in the dead of night and as the sun rose the villagers found mystery brickwork jutting out of the east coast sand.' It turned out to be some of the vestiges of what was the Manor House Hotel, which had slipped into the sea in the 1940s and had lain under the waves and sand until that storm. Tony Overill, Chairman of the Caister Parish Council, told the press, 'It's a phenomenon on this coast that whenever we get a strong north-easter it will scour the beach away.'

The hotel was very old, having been built in 1793 as a private house and becoming a hotel in 1894. In the 1920s, it was enlarged and had thirty-six bedrooms. It came up for sale in 1899, and the press description gives a good idea of what sort of hotel this was:

> The third portion of the Manor House Estate, well situate on high ground, on dry and healthy soil on the seafront in an open and rural position close to Caister railway station, within a walk of Great Yarmouth, close to the Caister and Yarmouth golf links; within easy reach of London, Norwich, Cromer, Sheringham and the Broads. Excellent site for seaside villas, for which there is a great and growing demand in the neighbourhood.

There is a photograph of the hotel, dated 1941, which shows that it was indeed a grand and impressive building. Its two levels and balcony on the upper floor, mock-Tudor gables and Elizabethan chimney, derivative of the famous architect Robert Smythson, make it solidly majestic and imposing.

All that remains of it now is a scattered array of brick fragments and scraps of metalwork on the sands. Tony Overill recalled that when he was a boy, he would wheel his bike along by the hotel, which was then derelict. He said that, after the initial fall, the last remains went in 1948.

In this area, south of Happisburgh, there have been changes that have demanded different strategies against the tides over the years. As J.C. Barringer explains in his edition of the Milne/Faden maps:

> Faden noted the changes in the nature of the coast south of Happisburgh from mud cliffs to the 'Marum hills' and he also carefully recorded nine breaches in the Marum Hills which had occurred up to the summer of 1792; this reminds us that the great floods of 1938 and 1953 were by no means the first on this stretch of coast.

One slight consolation here is that recent research has found that changes in erosion trends are very localised, and one report states: 'Coastline retreat followed by a period of relative stability typified trends at Caister-on-Sea between 1800 and 2007, whilst North Denes showed seaward advance after a period of erosion prior to 1890.' Locals at Caister must be praying that the next recession of the erosion process is just around the corner.

Yarmouth

Perhaps Ernest Suffling, in his book on the Broads, explained Yarmouth's beginnings:

> At the time of King Canute – according to ancient manuscripts – a large arm of the sea extended quite to Norwich; the Yare being at that period divided into two broad channels, which freely admitted the tides, over what are now meadows, quite up to the city. About the time of the Norman Conquest, one of these channels was gradually filled up by sand, and became solid ground, upon the most eastern portion of which the town of Yarmouth was built.

Back in the medieval times, the area of coast around Yarmouth was a series of havens: south of Caister was Grubbs Haven; north of Gorleston in a cluster were a second haven (granted by Richard II in 1392) and a fifth, alongside the Johnson haven, made in 1560; the fourth was by Hopton; the third (made in 1408) by Corton; and the first one, worked on as early as 1340, by Gunton. The early havens were not really protected by breakwaters or jetties. Something on a massive scale was needed, but of course, in those days, all works were ad hoc and piecemeal. As a town guide of 1959 explains, there were times of frustration across all these years of attempted building:

> When in 1508 it became obvious that yet another haven must be cut, a less persevering people would have despaired. All that is known of the site of this channel is that it was much nearer the town. This fared no better than its predecessors, for in 1529 yet another channel was being made – this time very near to the site of the existing haven – but once

again history repeated itself, and it was destroyed by wind and seas and the £15,000 spent on its construction was lost.

In the mid-Victorian years, the population of Yarmouth – the municipal borough – was around 42,000. By that time, it had become firmly established as a holiday destination. One handbook from the nineteenth century has, 'as a watering-place it is for the Eastern counties what Scarborough is for the Northern – the largest, the most frequented, the best supplied with resources for visitors, and the most overrun with excursionists in the summer.' At that time, Charles Dickens had done his bit for making the area better known by writing *David Copperfield*, published in serial form from 1849–50. In that novel, Dickens shows that he is aware of the threat of the sea, writing:

As we drew a little nearer and saw the whole adjacent prospect lying a straight low line under the sky, I hinted to Peggotty that a mound or so might have improved it; and also, that if the land had been a little more separated from the sea, and that the town and the tide had not been quite so much mixed up, like toast and water, it would have been nicer.

Traditionally, Yarmouth is said to have been made 'on herring bones'. But there was always a coal trade too, and the railway arrived to ensure the progress of the town as a holiday destination. The quay was always a main attraction, and one Victorian account stresses that it is 'a prominent and pleasant feature in the town ... above a mile long, and from 100 to 150 yards broad. It is planted with lime trees, and usually presents a busy and cheerful aspect.'

When Daniel Defoe went there in the 1720s, he found it 'beautiful' but commented on a defect:

though it is very rich and increasing in wealth and trade ... there is not room to enlarge the town by building, which would be certainly done much more than it is, but that the river on the land-side prescribes them.

Yet there is no doubt that he was impressed by the size, writing:

For the carrying on all these trades, they must have a very great number of ships, either of their own, or employed by them; and it may in some

measure be judged by this, that in the year 1697, I had an account from
the town register, that there was then 1,123 sail of ships.

While Yarmouth itself has had the investment, there is the old familiar story
of ruin at nearby Hopton beach. There, extensive damage has been done
by the sea, such as concrete walkways smashed and other wooden defences
damaged. There is one estimate that from 20,000 to 40,000 cubic metres
of sand has been lost from that beach per year. Expert opinions have been
called in and, for instance, one press report states, 'Coastal erosion expert
Dr Philip Barber studied the damage and his report concluded that the port
[Yarmouth] was to blame because of the changes in tidal flow and the littoral
drift.' This is exactly what has been found along the Yorkshire coast, where
the main seaside resorts have had the investment, and their solidity deflects
the wave action elsewhere and there is consequent erosion.

Gorleston

A photograph taken by Bernard Harris shows the ruin of the wall and beach
steps at Gorleston, and the internet provides a whole tranche of images of
crumbling cliffs and destruction done to defences around the area. A century
ago, one witness told the press, 'Speaking generally, the sea gradually takes
away portions of land every year, but considerably more has gone during the
last three years.' Clearly, there is a problem.

It looks as though the future here is going to be a repeat of events at
Happisburgh or at Easton Bavents.

In *Kelly's Directory* of 1883, Gorleston is noted for its gasworks and the
herring fishery; the author seemed to have no reason for drawing attention
to any coastal erosion. It was a parish suburb of Yarmouth with a population
of 9,008 in the 1881 census. It had been annexed to Yarmouth back in 1681.
It has remained an attractive holiday venue, and the only drawback is the
relentless assault on its shoreline. But at least there has been the occasional
element of humour in this, such as the story in 2003 when a huge rock was
exposed by the sea, bearing some strange inscriptions. Was it a rare find
with runic lettering? Some thought so, but then a man confessed to having
done the patterns very recently. The rock had been one of an importation of
massive rocks as revetments against the tides.

Chapter 5

Suffolk Places Lost and Threatened

It is a suitable climate for a little arable kingdom where flints are the jewels
and where existence is sharp-edged.

Ronald Blythe, *Akenfield*

Sandlands

I am going to use the term 'Sandlands' as I venture into the story of the
Suffolk coast, as that is the most appropriate term for this land. In his
book, *Sandlands: The Suffolk Coast and Heaths* (2005), Tom Williamson
explains that this land has long had its own name – sometimes *Sandlands*
and sometimes *Sandlings*. A study of the map of that area shows just how
near the inland communities are to water, as the long and substantial rivers
cut in from the sea. The heathland, the sandy soil and the areas that have
benefitted from afforestation give the whole tract an attractive variety, but
that geography also adds some clues as to how the sea and its destruction-
creation cycles has radically changed the terrain over the centuries. My
following descriptions offer merely summaries of the sea's work at the key
locations down the coast. A guide to Suffolk from the 1950s gives the clearest
descriptions of this coast:

> It only needs a glance at any old map of the county to realise how the
> coastline has altered its shape. The inroads of the North Sea have not
> only eaten away large portions of land and built up in at least one place,
> Hollesley Bay, a long bank of shingle, but have also played curious tricks
> with the rivers as they approach the sea. There were at one time along
> this coast, flourishing towns, such as Walton with its great castle, which
> have been entirely engulfed by the sea.

The fundamental geographical fact about Suffolk's coast is that the tides come from the north, carrying the shingle, which will mostly stay and form barriers and banks, so therefore harbour bars will accrete, and they will become prominent features of the land. As Lilian Redstone pointed out in her guide to the county, written almost ninety years ago, this has caused disputes and oppositions. She wrote that 'Yarmouth quarrelled with Gorleston because the harbour shifted thither, and Southwold disputed with Dunwich, and each town tried to cut through the bar to make itself a direct harbour from the sea.' She also pointed out how some of the worst erosion occurred: 'Yarmouth made itself so good a protection against the shingle from the north piled up, that shingle defences no longer formed ... and the sea began to eat into the land between Yarmouth and Lowestoft.'

Seaside piers are an important aspect of the social history of this part of the coast. Since Edwardian times, postcards have shown the piers at the main resorts. Similarly, piers on the Yorkshire coast illustrated the pros and cons of such enterprises. Norfolk's outstanding example is Cromer Pier. Built in 1901, it was for many years the town's main attraction, and four years after opening, its bandstand was covered over to make a pavilion. Its later history is entirely typical of the fate of so many British piers: thrashed and buffeted by gales and storms, as well as being rammed by a barge, it was in serious trouble, and was rebuilt in 1955.

Piers are beautiful installations, today being celebrated and preserved by the National Piers Society. In earlier times, they were seen as one of the strategies against the advance of the sea. Unfortunately, they come with a negative element, as they cause shingle to gather and cause deflections of the tides, so that other areas may be affected. This is explained by experts in the subject when answering the question as to what effect piers and trestles may have on erosion processes:

The supporting piles may have an impact on coastal processes ... especially if the number of piles is rather large and with large diameters of the piles ... obliquely arriving waves will cause an area with reduced wave heights in the lee of the structure ... spots of some accretion may occur.

So, there is a down side to that wonderful sight of the pier, where visitors stroll and the band plays on. Piers will always be popular, but the days are gone when they might be seen as tools in the war against the assaults of the waves.

Around Lowestoft

In the few miles around the Lowestoft area, Corton is the place that has caught the attention of the drama-seeking press, because coastal erosion there has been extreme. It has a long history, having been the site of a Roman signal station, and later it was in the deanery of Lothingland. In Domesday it is shown as having two cobs, five cattle, twelve pigs, fifty sheep and wood for three pigs. Enclosures took place in 1814, with 236 acres being enclosed. From 1760 to the end of that century, about 1,500 private Enclosure Acts were passed. This was the general trend for open land to be enclosed and fenced by land owners, in order to maximise profits from agriculture or from animal pasture. Naturally, this caused widespread social unrest, as ordinary people lost rights of grazing and food gathering from the enclosed areas.

In a gazetteer of 1868, among the basic facts we find this: 'The sea is gradually encroaching upon the cliffs, and has swept away an entire parish, called Newton.' It was always the old way home for the trawlermen, and the Corton light was well known to all. An ancient rhyme sums up the feeling of seeing the place:

> *When you come to Corton*
> *The way begins to shorten.*

We are fortunate in having a rare oral history record referring to this lost parish, from A.E. Bensley:

Sometime in the mid 1960s a heavy storm, accompanied by a scouring sea struck our coastline. After the sea abated, my wife Carol and I went for a walk along the shore. Reaching the area where the village [Newton] would have stood, we were amazed to find literally hundreds of what appeared to be blackened animal bones, plus timbers in the same condition; these had obviously been beneath the sea-silt for hundreds of years. We did not identify any human remains and had that been the case we would have notified the authorities.'

More recently, Lowestoft has had a bad press in the works of one of East Anglia's most highly rated authors, the late W.G. Sebald, who lectured at the University of East Anglia and wrote innovative prose that mixes travel writing with fiction. In his book *The Rings of Saturn*, he – or his narrator – visits Lowestoft, and the reader is given a bleak picture:

> The last time I had been in Lowestoft was perhaps fifteen years ago, on a June day that I spent on the beach with two children, and I thought I remembered a town that had become something of a backwater but was nonetheless very pleasant; so now, as I walked into Lowestoft, it seemed incomprehensible to me that ... the place could have become so run down.

Guidebooks produced in the 1950s, when Lowestoft was growing as a seaside destination, said quite the opposite. One of these has: 'The sea breezes are rarely cold even in winter and in summer they present excessive heat ... the town stands high in the list of resorts experiencing maximum sunshine.'

Of course, having two parades and a pier, with Belle Vue Park 80 feet above the sea, the place was always going to be popular. Close by is Oulton Broad, home of the writer George Borrow and also a place of water sports, with gentle cruising on wherries and relaxation in cafés and bars. A travel handbook of 1892 stresses the main attractions: 'Lowestoft, in Suffolk, is a high-class watering place. It is noted for being one of the most favoured Health Resorts in the kingdom. Its well appointed hotels and numerous lodging houses afford excellent accommodation to visitors.' This is quite the opposite of Sebald's image of a run-down and depressing place.

In the Domesday Book Lowestoft is recorded as having sixteen households; there were three families, ten smallholders and three slaves. It was part of the Hundred of Lothingland. Of course, being subject to flooding, it was hit very hard in the tremendous floods of 1953, the southern part of the town being the worst affected. More recently, there have been breaches made by the sea: in the surge of 2013, extensive damage was done, such as the Children's Corner construction and the sea wall. After that, part of the beach was closed and one report stressed the dramatic appearance of the 'old sea defences' composed of 'debris which littered the beach'. Now 6,000 tons of rock has been placed as beach protection, and part of the sea wall had to be protected for some time by security fencing. The Environment Agency is spending £2 million pounds on repair work.

A survey of the area around Lowestoft reveals that Pakefield is one of the locations most affected by the sea. In 1941, travel writer Arthur Mee wrote of it:

> The older it grows the smaller it gets. Since the beginning of this century nearly a hundred of its houses and part of the village green have dropped into the sea, and the church which used to be half a mile away is now only 80 yards from the cliff. Low tide discloses that ages ago the sea swallowed up a forest here and we talked to men who have ploughed and harvested fields now covered with sand and drowned at high tide. Some of the fishermen have faced their cottage walls with pebbles from the beach.

Mee would surely have known that the flint used in house building across East Anglia would have the distinctive feature he mentions here, but still, he was stressing the closeness of the fishing communities to the sea that destroyed them. He summed up his response to the place with, 'Pakefield ... drops a house or two every year.'

Today it is described as a suburb of Lowestoft, but over the centuries, and up to the early twentieth century, it was a parish. It has made the headlines, notably so in 2005, when an archaeological dig revealed remains of early man living in the area. It has now the distinction of being the location of the oldest identified human dwellings anywhere in Britain. The human species discovered there has been dated to 700,000 years ago. Later, there was a Romano-British settlement and evidence of the first phase of the Viking era in Britain.

In Domesday it was *Pagefella*, referring to 'Pagga's field', and it was part of the hundred of Lothing. That record notes seventeen households. Obviously, from those early times to today, there has been a steady rate of erosion. But along with so many other small communities along the 'Sandlands' coast of Suffolk, it has emerged as a holiday destination.

We know something about the social history of the town from an unusual source: the poet Edward FitzGerald, who lived for many years in Woodbridge, had a fascination with the sea and the lives of sailors and fishermen. He went to Lowestoft in 1859 to stay for several months, and while there he got to know the seamen who were mostly hanging around, with very little money, out of the fishing season. Through his eyes the reader becomes acquainted with these men, and his biographer Robert Martin explains the interest he felt:

> He particularly liked to look of the herring fishermen who 'really half-starve here during the winter', but he admired all the 'beachmen', as they were known, for their 'half-starving independence' and their 'wonderful shoulders: won't take one out in one of their yawls for a sovereign though they will give one a ride when they go out to get nothing at all.' It was their very simplicity and nearness to the primitive that so attracted FitzGerald.

These are the men who would have occupied those homes near to the sea, the ones washed off the beach as recorded in the memoirs of people such as James Maggs. FitzGerald came to know the locals very well, and in a letter to his friend W.A. Wright, he wrote:

> I have never heard ... here or elsewhere of the 'shoulder of sail', an apt phrase, which Shakespeare might have originated, as if born and bred to the craft. I will enquire, however, from Lowestoft friends, when I go that way.

Kessingland

The novelist H. Rider Haggard was a landholder as well as the famous author of *King Solomon's Mines*, and he kept a journal of his life as a farmer and justice of the peace in Norfolk. One of his pieces of land was in Kessingland, and he wrote accounts on the place with very full information. He was also a man of strong social and political views and incorporated such expressions into his journal. Here he begins by logging damage done, referring to the 1890s:

> Never has such a time for high tides been known, and the gale of December last will long be remembered on the east coast for its terrible amount of damage. The sight close to a house which I possess at Kessingland, a place near Lowestoft, was something to remember, for here and at Pakefield the high cliff has been taken away by the thousand tons. In such a tide the fierce scour from the north licks the sand cliff and hollows it out till the clay stratum above it falls, and is washed into the ocean. Fortunately for me, my house is protected by a sea wall and though the water got behind this, it did no further damage.... The old residents on the coast declare that no such tide has been known within the present century.

Rider Haggard then assumes the role of local lecturer and moralist:

> For generations the sea has been encroaching on this coast. So long ago as the time of Queen Elizabeth it is said that three churches went over the cliff at Dunwich in a single Sunday afternoon, yet during all this time no concerted effort has been made for the common protection.... If we were Dutchmen the matter would have been different, but here in rural England, unless they are forced to it by Act of Parliament, it is almost impossible to oblige people to combine to win future profits or ward off future dangers.

Later, in 1898, he wrote again of a storm just after Christmas, and took a wider view:

> But a gale from the south-west is not that which does damage on the eastern coast – it is the nor'easter we dread, especially if accompanied by high tides. This was what happened in the great storm of last December, when the tide and the sea rose higher than they are believed to have done for the best part of a century. The damage at Lowestoft, Southwold, Pakefield etc. was enormous.

His Kessingland in the mid-Victorian years was certainly under assault from the sea, continually and savagely. *The National Gazetteer* noted in 1868 that 'the old town walls are embedded in the sand' and the *Post Office Directory* three years earlier gave a very useful historical perspective:

> This was anciently a place of considerable importance, having a weekly market, and a fair on the 20th November. The sea, however, is making its encroachments upon the land: a piece of land known as 'Sea Row', a place thickly populated, was swept away about thirty years since by the action of the waves: two walls then standing, which remained like turrets in the sand.

In the 1860s, inhabitants included plenty of farmers, a few shopkeepers, tradesmen and a beer retailer. Notably, one farmer was a Miss Mary Crowfoot.

Covehithe

Arthur Mee commented on Covehithe, 'South of the woods and water of Benacre Broad, half a mile from the sea, lies this small place, overshadowed by a mighty ruin. ... It is Covehithe's medieval church, which the villagers destroyed late in the seventeenth century.'

James Maggs, an auctioneer, kept a diary for many years during the mid-nineteenth century. One of his entries for 1848 concerns Covehithe, but on this occasion it was the wind that did the damage, not the sea:

> Barn belonging to Mr Edmund Cottingham at Covehithe, a tenant of Sir Thomas Gooch, catches fire. A north-east gale blowing, it was reduced to ashes in two hours. The exertions of labourers from Covehithe and Southwold and the Southwold fire engine save the threatened farm.

There are several points of interest here: first, Covehithe was open and vulnerable to weather of the worst kind. Gales and sea, and, of course, sand, were constant enemies; then there is the pulling together, the impressive common cause and self-help; finally, there is the note that help came from some kind of fire service. In 1848 that was a rare event, anywhere.

Today, the tarmac road leads right to the cliff edge. In 1780, the coastline was 150 metres further out than today; now the church, a ruin, is placed only about 400 metres from the cliff edge.

Southwold

Again, Arthur Mee, the inveterate traveller and chronicler of provincial England in the 1930s, has something significant to say about Southwold:

> Half of it lies in the sea, and no man can say when the waves will swallow up the other half of old Southwold; yet it has been a prosperous place since the days of Edward the Confessor, when its fishermen paid 20,000 herrings every year to the lord of the manor.

Around 1850, the population was roughly 2,700. It was becoming a place where people went for the improvement of their health. But all was not well with the working inhabitants; one local newspaper feature for 1851 remarked that the able bodied labourers were in a poor condition and referred to 'destitute farmers'. Not long before that, as Christopher Crayon recalled, writing about growing up in Suffolk in the 1820s, 'The coastal parts of East Suffolk were terribly isolated in those days. There was plenty of opportunity for the growth of local prejudice and eccentricity.' He also noted that the highlight of the day was the sight of the mail coach. He wrote, 'Gross darkness covered the land in that pre-scientific age. Life was stagnant in a post-war depression.' That was thirty years before the beginnings of the place as a destination for travellers wanting rest and sea air.

The record of wrecks and losses of vessels at sea off Southwold is alarmingly high. James Maggs, in his dairy in February 1848, noted a typical occurrence: 'Southwold lifeboat rescues the crew of nine from the brig *Cleofrid* of Newcastle, driven on to Sizewell bank during a gale.' In the same year we have this:

> Southwold lifeboat goes out to the vessel of and from Sunderland, sailing to Dunkirk, which dismasted during a heavy gale from the south-west, was driven on to the northern part of the Barnard Sand

on Monday, 4 December 1848. Sighted from Kessingland, a messenger was despatched on horseback to Southwold. Two men rescued and taken to Lowestoft, where they were lodged at the Suffolk Hotel.

Maggs's diary also gives us a chronicle of the sea's advances around Southwold. His notes and descriptions provide the full range of sea incursions in all their rich variety, from gales whipping up the waves, to floods and harbour problems.

In early 1853 we have an account of an assault by the sea that includes specific names and places:

> The sea at intervals ... has made alarming inroads opposite the Gun Hill and as far to the north as the Long Island Cliff, scarcely leaving sufficient width for the standing of the bathing machines opposite the houses of Miss Sheriffe – the ground and flag pole in front of the New York Cliff house are all gone except of about four and a half feet – the Watch House – belonging to the Coast Guard is so undermined that it is expected hourly to fall.... The path which leads to the Gun Hill opposite the house belonging to Mr Delf is gone, exposing the gas pipes so much so as the Gas Company was obliged immediately to remove them.

Regarding the Watch House, he adds later, 'It fell down 9 May 1864. I saw it.' He also gives a note on Mr Delf's house, which is of real interest, explaining that in 1816 the distance from his lawn to the cliff edge was 62 feet, and in 1853 this was reduced to only 40 feet.

In 1855, there was a strong wind and a high tide, resulting in allotments on the Haven marshes being flooded, and once again, Gun Hill suffered damage. A year later, Robert Winter's house, known as Cobbold's, which was on the beach, was 'partly washed down', and he adds, 'No person living ever saw the beach in the state it is now.' In 1862, the press reported that there was damage to the lifeboat house, the sailor's reading room, the government boathouse and two fishermen's cottages on the coast.

One of the very worst gales and floods reported in the years of Maggs's diary was in early 1863. This gale shattered the homes of many of the fishermen:

Sadly altered is the beach where the picturesque old fishing huts and homes of the fishermen clustered under the cliff, doubtless fondly remembered by many a one ... and who will remember the civility and attention of a 'Sam Waters' or the long yarns of a 'David Simpson'.

He concluded that 'Nothing is now left between the sea and the cliff.'

The reading room is a very significant detail here. This was the age in which several institutions were developing popular reading matter, along with regular 'Penny Readings' at such places as mechanics' institutes and Masonic halls; the relation of seamen to self-education and popular culture is referenced here, and the loss of the reading room was a major issue. In fact, in June 1864, Maggs notes that a new one had been built and was opened. He retained a press cutting noting that a new reading room and cottage was contracted, and the work soon completed.

More recently, the writer W.G. Sebald has visited and written about that reading room, and he also sat on the same Gun Hill. He makes a point of lifting the description to quite lyrical, melancholy heights, as it is such a survival from the past – reclaimed, as it were, from the tides of time, 'a charitable establishment housed in a small building above the promenade, which nowadays, sailors being a dying breed, serves principally as a kind of maritime museum.'

A very typical Suffolk issue arises in his entry for October 1853: the neglect of the river channel and silting. Maggs quotes a newspaper cutting that reported on a meeting of the Southwold Harbour Commissioners, which was held at the Old Swan. At that meeting reference was made to the 'chronic disease' the port was subject to, expressed in these words: 'The neglected state of the channel of the river navigation between Reydon quay and Bulcamp lock is the great evil of the port.' Three years later he noted that the harbour was 'blocked up' and, 'The London stage coach, Blue Rous, attempted to drive across on his way to Ipswich – prevented by [a] small channel at the south or back of the south pier.'

Matters went from bad to worse, and there was a public meeting in June 1856 to protest against 'the present state of the harbour'. Much earlier, in late Elizabethan times, an outlet was cut by local workers. There was a very old church located at the edge of the marshland, and this was finally lost in

1728. The general changes in the location of Walberswick being eastwards of the old church. A guide to the new church of St Andrew, printed in the 1980s, notes that a series of charters gave the town its trade in a variety of produce: 'Here a considerable trade was done in butter, cheese, bacon, corn, timber, coals, salt and fish, principally the last.'

In the Domesday Book, parish churches at both Walberswick and Blythborough were named.

Easton Bavents

Over the course of history, nobody has particularly noticed the little community of Easton Bavents, near Southwold. A reference work of 1868 stated:

> This place, which is by antiquaries identified with the *Extensio* of Ptolemy [a Roman geographer], was formerly the most eastern point of land in the kingdom; but the promontory called Easton Ness has long since been washed away by the sea, which has made great encroachments on this part of the coast; and the church and an ancient chapel, with the greater portion of the parish, have disappeared.

The same work thought it to be a 'picturesque' place. There is a grand irony – that such beauty would be allowed to be erased, as is the modern situation.

One useful record in the history of the shrinking of the place comes from the accounts books of a man called John Hopton, the owner of the manor in the troubled times of the Wars of the Roses. These contain a note on a tenant called Wiseman who had less to pay because he had lost some of his land from erosion and slippage. Tom Williamson refers to this in his book on the Sandlands: 'Parts of the manorial demesne were also being eaten away: between 1464 and 1465, one piece of land, 4½ acres in extent, was reduced by an acre.'

It is known that at some time in the mid-seventeenth century, the church of St Nicholas and the main village were washed away, along with a chapel dedicated to St Margaret. This was to the west of the church and tradition has it that this chapel was where a particularly special holy relic was housed.

Therefore it must have been a pilgrimage site, and records show that at the very end of its life, up to around the 1740s, it was being used as a barn. At the height of the Middle Ages, there would have been a thriving community, with a weekly market and an annual fair.

The chronicle of coastal erosion on the east coast, as the reader will now be fully aware, offers marked contrasts between those places without backing and finance and those places with ample resources. But individuals still come out and fight; after all, this book is about England. One such commando in the war against both the sea and authority is Peter Boggis. He has been described as a 'gallant knight battling for the right of all Englishmen to defend their homes against the encroaching sea'. According to one press feature, he spent £400,000 making his own clay barriers to keep his house safe.

At the heart of his protest, and his direct action, is, in addition to his own property being saved, the fact that he lives in an area that is defined as a Site of Special Scientific Interest. As noted in a feature by Will Pavis, this scientific element comes from the challenging fact that it is 'in the interests of science to allow the ground beneath his home to erode naturally'.

In 2008, Mr Boggis won his action against Natural England and the move to let nature destroy the land. He told the press: 'I'm fighting in the interests of everyone who lives on the coast of England.' A High Court judge, Mr Justice Blair, ruled that the argument of Natural England – that the cliffs be allowed to slip – was not acceptable, and that Mr Boggis's plea that he be allowed to save his home using his own barrier be upheld. The Suffolk man had used 250,000 tons of compacted clay as the cliff defence. Mr Justice Blair also thought that allowing the cliffs to crumble would have an undesirable effect on the ecology of the area, particularly the bird life. There was also a legal element, because the judge stated that there had not been an appropriate assessment by Natural England in line with the EU Habitats Directive.

In 2009, an appeal by Natural England overturned the verdict. The fight goes on, with Mr Boggis in the role of crusader for home and land protection. But there are other stories, too. David Horne, in a feature for the local press, was interviewed and some memories were gathered of more Easton Bavents history. One man said that 'in a lifetime, forty houses have been lost to the sea together with an isolation hospital. This is marked on a 1937 map. ... It is south of Cox's Farm. Also the map shows a rifle range, or "The Butts".' The author also adds a memory from another local man: 'My great-grandfather, who was a skipper of a steam drifter, lived in a little cottage at Covehithe, which is about half a mile out to sea now.

Mr Boggis was interviewed on television in 2016 for the BBC series *Coast*. The film showed what had been a familiar sight on the stretch of coast beneath where Nicholas Crane and Mr Boggis were standing as they spoke: a continuous movement of huge lorries bringing material from building sites, which they dropped and flattened to layer a band of cliff defence. This has now had to stop (as I write this in late 2016) because of a court action. Mr Boggis told Nicholas Crane: 'If it were feasible for me to start again, without fear of legal action, I would do it without compunction.' They looked down on 500 metres of beach that in the past had seen fifty trucks a day dumping soil and gravel on the sand.

That tireless maker of maps in the Jacobean times, John Speed produced a map in 1610 that shows the position of the church, and next to where the words 'Easton Bavents' are printed, there is a distinctive headland, with the symbol for the church by the side.

Walberswick

This place is named after a Saxon called Waldbert or perhaps Walhbert, and the full name is modernised as 'Walbert's harbour'. Back in Saxon times, the curve of the river Blyth made a harbour (a *wic*). This Saxon area did very well, and after the Norman Conquest, in the thirteenth century the place received its first charter, followed by others up to the early seventeenth century. These were concerned with easing taxation, and it is in such matters from the past that we might begin to understand the rivalry and jealousies that developed around the area, with Dunwich, Walberswick and Blythburgh being involved.

As the website for the Walberswick Local History group explains: 'These charters gave Walberswick relief from tolls and taxes which in turn gave the inhabitants a great advantage over neighbouring settlements.' The confrontations and disagreements eventually led to actions taken by Henry IV in 1408, insisting that Dunwich could not apply tolls.

The three places all had problems with the sea. The issues were related to silting, the usual problem; of course, the silt formed banks that prevented or at least severely limited the usual shipping from navigating the area. The result was the shrinking of Walberswick as fishing declined.

A key date in Walberswick history, as with almost all of the British east coast, is 1953, the year of the severe floods. The Walberswick Local History Group has printed an account by Miss Browton, who kept a diary at the time, and this includes an incident that was replicated along the coast:

> A family consisting of a mother and three small children had to be evacuated from their cottage with the aid of a boat from their bedroom window and it was a sad sight for days afterwards, when furniture and goods were carried on to the green to dry.

Dunwich

Mr Maggs, with whom the reader is now well acquainted, went to Dunwich with his friend Mr Gooding in March 1857. Once again, his diary entry gives particular information:

> The sea so much encroached here – from the East end of church to edge of cliff 45 feet – several feet of churchyard gone – human bones continually falling out of graves into the sea – at the bottom of the cliff at low water is the bottom of a well about 3 or 4 feet deep – the top of it was on the top of the cliff and was at the least 50 feet deep – Mr Dix's house which stood at least 100 yards from the edge is now only 7 yards.

Chapter 6 tells the full story of the town, but in this context, this is the ideal place to mention the early history. In AD 731, Bede wrote his great *History of the English Church and People*, in which he recounts the life of St Felix. In the course of the events recalled, he wrote this:

> He delivered the entire province from its age-old wickedness and infelicity, brought it to the Christian faith and works of righteousness and ... guided it towards eternal felicity. His Episcopal see was

established at Dunwich; and after ruling the province as its bishop for seventeen years, he ended his days there in peace.

The word Bede actually used for Dunwich was 'Dommoc' and there is still some debate about whether or not this was Dunwich or another place, perhaps Walton, near Felixstowe.

Rowland Parker, whose book *Men of Dunwich* is the fullest account we have of this disappeared town, notes that 'the case for Felix at Dunwich is pretty strong.... This bishopric was definitely there in AD 673, possibly having been removed from Felixstowe [on account of marine erosion?].'

Before Felix it was a Roman port: the place the Romans called *Sitomagus* may have been Dunwich. So once again, looking at the place in its early phase of growth is problematic. I will return to the town in much more detail later, but regarding its place at the point at which it had fairly recently been lost in almost its entirety, there is no one better than Defoe, writing in the 1720s, to prepare the modern reader for what is surely the most astounding and dramatic of all the stories of towns lost to the North Sea:

for fame reports that once they had fifty churches in the town; I saw but one left, and that not half full of people. This town is a testimony to the decay of public things, things of the most durable nature; and as the old poet expressed it, by numerous examples we may see, that towns and cities die, as well as we.

The ruins of Carthage, or the great city of Jerusalem, are not at all as wonderful to me, the ruins of Nineveh, which are entirely sunk ... these I say are not at all wonderful, because being the capitals of great and flourishing kingdoms ... the capital cities necessarily fell with them. But for a private town, a sea-port, and a town of commerce, to decay as it were of itself ... this I must confess seems owing to nothing but the fate of things.

By the side of all the other tales of places that have disintegrated and fallen into the waves, Dunwich stands alone as a place that we may still envisage as being out there, in the bay off what is now left. People may stand and stare, and imagine what lies beneath that pool of water, behind the easy lapping of the insistent waves, with their steady rhythm, marking time, and yet somehow timeless. Defoe trod on ground that is now no longer there.

This brief preface to an account of the lost town must suffice as an invitation to the reader to consider not merely a dropped church or even a beach of huts and cottages blown away or engulfed, but a whole town. It is the closest instance we have here to that other icon of disappearance and rather eerie nothingness, the village swamped by the reservoir, known to be lying under the placid water as people walk or cycle by at their leisure.

Thorpeness

The recent bulletins from management agencies, reporting after the horrendous storms of 2013, are reassuring to the people living in the row of colourful houses arranged along the shingle beach at Thorpeness. Damage happens there, it seems, but the gabions and revetments are doing their job. It is a popular holiday venue, its history in that respect perhaps being dominated by Glencairn Ogilvie, a lawyer who developed the place, creating a country club and much more.

Nature has given Thorpeness the 'Meare' also, an artificial lake in which the writer J.M. Barrie had a certain influence. In terms of tourism, the attractions of Thorpeness are in its offering a quiet holiday with a particular identity – colourful and memorable, not least because of the 'House in the Clouds' – a converted water tower that of course is unmissable on the skyline.

As usual in the case of coastal erosion, there is a reliance on those who actually walk the land in question, and in this case, the blogspot 'Griffmaster' offers some local knowledge: 'The Suffolk Coast Path has been re-routed from Sizewell to Thorpeness.' But it can still be walked when the tide is favourable to movement, it seems.

Aldeburgh

It is difficult for locals to take comfort from the professional geologists' view that the stretch of coast between Dunwich and Benacre is characterised by material being deposited rather than being eroded. Yet that appears to be the case. The other general characteristic here is that, as Tom Williamson has

put it, 'coastal erosion is ... an episodic rather than a continuous process.'
Williamson takes Aldeburgh as his template for this line of thought, as he
explains that it has had episodic retreat. That is, for long periods after severe
erosion, there is no geomorphological change. He quotes a Tudor map that
shows in the centre of the town three parallel streets, whereas a 1787 survey
shows just two streets there. He adds: 'the market-place and moot hall, which
had earlier stood in the centre of the town [are] now standing beside the beach.'

H. Alker Tripp, already referred to as a sailor who knew these coasts,
summed up the Aldborough he saw in the 1920s:

> Aldeburgh, in the greyness, lay abeam, a low line of houses on the
> shingly shore. Its life is now that of a mere seaside resort; its significance
> to the trade and enterprise of Suffolk has vanished. Lying on the 'dead'
> coast, it is a useful example of the changed aspect of things. In 1590,
> Aldeburgh had twenty-four fishing boats of 20 tons, Walberswick
> and Dunwich had seven each, Southwold three, Lowestoft two. Now
> Lowestoft has some 490 fishing vessels between 20 and 200 tons, and
> Aldeburgh none.

There is a very telling insight into the coastal problems of this area in a
statement made to the Royal Commission on Coastal Erosion in 1911. This
came from a landowner called Stradbrooke from Wangford:

> I own some marshes reclaimed over 100 years ago and I have to keep
> up the river wall; last year it cost me over £200 topping it and filling
> up weak places; if I let the wall down the sea would flood the reclaimed
> marshes and several hundred acres of low-lying marshes besides, also
> the London road between Blythburgh and Bulcamp, about half a mile,
> and it would flow up the road by Wolsey bridge, Reydon; but this road
> being raised, it would only be covered at exceptionally high tides.

It is one of those footnotes of history that shows how everything is inter-
dependent; the water being hemmed in where there is reclamation brings
with it further problems, and a study of the coast necessarily enlarges to
cover the incursions into farmlands further inland and upriver.

Aldeburgh is known for many reasons, but one of the most celebrated local stories is that the poet George Crabbe was from that town. In his poem *The Borough* he wrote at length on the sea and life at its edge, including these lines on the terror that the sea may bring:

> *From parted clouds the moon her radiance throws*
> *On the wild waves, and all the danger shows;*
> *But shows them beaming in her shining vest,*
> *Terrific splendour! Gloom in glory dressed!*
> *This for a moment, and then clouds again*
> *Hide every beam, and fear and darkness reign.*

Crabbe's life and writings provide a great deal of useful information about the place. One of his first biographers, Rene Huchon, writing in the 1960s, researched the town at that time and his account gives some excellent insights into its relationship with the sea. Crabbe was born on Christmas Eve, 1754, and as Huchon puts it, he 'belonged to a family which was too obscure to possess history'. Huchon looked briefly into the Crabbe history and summarised: 'The southern part of the county of Norfolk seems to have been their favourite residence; at the end of the seventeenth century the Crabbes probably lived in the little parish of Seething.' But Crabbe's grandfather moved to Aldborough and there he worked as Collector of Customs.

Huchon gives a very vivid account of the town c. 1960:

The traveller who visits Aldborough today can hardly recognise the village or the borough described by Crabbe. Since the beginning of the last century the population has nearly trebled, and the occupations of the inhabitants have changed. The fishing boats moored to the shore are now few and far between; Slaughden Quay, on which the custom house formerly stood and where Crabbe and his father toiled as simple labourers, still exists. ... The direct line of railway between London and Yarmouth has monopolised the traffic of this part of the world.

This picture does not touch on the past losses to the sea, but Huchon fulfils the role of historian as well as that of biographer, and gives a clear account of the chronicle of erosion and flood:

> Nature herself seems to have become more civilised. As if weary of having stormed this luckless coast for so many years, of having insensibly scooped out the slight curve of the bay of which Aldborough occupies the centre, the sea has raised against its own fury a rampart of shingle.

This is the primary impression the visitor today has: Aldborough as a great stretch of pebble beach, with the huts and then the parallel line of shops and hotels behind.

Its past had indeed been violent, and it has been intensively assaulted by the ocean. As Huchon puts it:

> At low tide the receding waves lay bare a strip of close, fine sand. . . . When walking on it one would never suspect that the sea has swallowed up the ruins of perhaps the most populous quarter of Aldborough 300 years ago, and that the quaint old town hall an advanced sentinel facing the ocean, that solitary Moot Hall, almost tottering on foundations of less breadth than its first and only storey.

He understands the landscape he saw almost fifty years ago and notes that the sandbank is the most significant feature here, as when he describes the river Alde, 'at about 200 yards from the shore it encounters a narrow strip of land, or shingle rather, which deflects it abruptly towards the south and it has to flow alongside the sea for 12 miles.'

Crabbe himself gave us very powerful descriptions of the area, one of the most general and evocative being:

> *But few our acres, and but short our grass;*
> *In some fat pastures of the rich, indeed,*
> *May roll the single cow or favourite steed;*
> *But these, our hilly heath and common wide,*
> *Yield a slight portion.*

Orford and Orford Ness

When Daniel Defoe passed this way in the 1720s, he immediately saw the effects that the sea had had over the centuries, and it was crystal clear to him that here land was accreting:

> Orford was once a good town, but is decayed, and as it stands on the land-side of the river, the sea daily throws up more land to it, and falls off itself from it, as if it were resolved to disown the place, and that it should be a seaport no longer.

This provides the clearest description, for the layperson, outside the geology books, as to how the silting and marsh formation occurs all the way down the East Anglian coast; the same issue was described at King's Lynn, and down through all the offshore sandbanks and shingle banks that have been formed by longshore drift. Defoe saw the bright side of this when looking at Orford Ness, of course, where the long spit provided, as he saw, 'a noted point of land for the colliers and coasters'.

Arguably, the most prominent loss to the sea here was the first castle, preceding the one Henry II began to build in 1165. As one of Henry's biographers commented, 'Henry's castle strategy is well illustrated in his dealings with Hugh Bigod, Earl of Norfolk.' Bigod was a very powerful man at this time, and he had three castles in Suffolk – Framlingham, Bungay and Walton. He had sided with the Angevins in the struggles for power during and after Stephen's reign of anarchy. Bigod had a violent feud with William of Blois, and Henry deprived them of castles in a move to exert control and stem the tide of yet more internecine strife. Bigod was given back his property, as long as he paid a fine. With all this turmoil in the background, it is no surprise that Henry built a strong new castle at Orford.

From time to time in maritime history, something that may only be described as folklore crops up, and this is always related to the special relationship of fishing communities to the sea. That relationship has given rise to shanties, folksong and poetry, as well as artefacts in the practical arts and also paintings, but few of these are as strange as the 'Wild Man' of Orford. The tale was reported in Murray's *Handbook* of 1875:

A curious story relating to Orford, is told by Ralph Coggeshall (abbot of the monastery there in the early part of the thirteenth century). Some fishermen on this coast (AD 1161) caught in their nets one stormy day a monster resembling a man in size and form, bald-headed, but with a long beard. It was taken to the governor of Orford Castle, and kept for some time, being fed on raw fish and flesh, which it 'pressed with its hands' before eating. The soldiers in the castle used to torture the unhappy monster in divers [*sic*] fashions 'to make him speak', and on one occasion, when it was taken into the sea to disport itself therein, it broke through a triple barrier of nets and escaped. Strange to say, not long afterwards it returned of its own accord to its captivity; but at last, 'being wearied of living alone, it stole away to sea and was never more heard of.'

In more recent times, Orford Ness has been of great interest because of its military connections. Wartime installations have been prominent, including a top-secret base involved in Cold War defence and planning.

But there is one Orford story that typifies the very essence of the sea threat. It relates to the lighthouse, a 100-foot high red and white banded tower, which has been there since 1792. It is now very close to the sea, and local people are anxious to save it. In the last four years (2012–16) the distance of the lighthouse from the sea has halved. Nick Gold and other local folk have been doing all they can to retain the shingle beach, even filling huge bags with pebbles, which they can use to weigh down and retain the base of shingle. There are other reasons for keeping the Ness as it is, the least of which is the preservation of the wildlife there, which includes over 200 species of birds. It looks as though Nick Gold and his group are having some success in their struggle against the waves.

Walton and Felixstowe

There is much more to Felixstowe than freight containers and long stretches of busy waterfront crowded with labourers. For one thing, its name will always suggest Felix, the bishop, whose impact on Suffolk in the post-Roman years was profound.

When Defoe came by this area in the 1720s, it was Walton he noticed – it was the most prominent. He wrote:

> At Walton ... they find on the shore, copperas-stone in great quantities; and there are several large works called Copperas Houses, where they make it with great expense. The sea gains so much upon the land here, by the continual winds at SW that within the memory of some, they have lost above 30 acres of land in some places.

Far back in the Domesday Book, Walton only was mentioned – not Felixstowe – and even then, it consisted of merely a few clifftop homes.

This refers to the production of green vitriol (also called ferrous sulphate), which is Defoe's 'Copperas'. This was a valuable industry because the material was used for inks and dyes, and there was also the creation of sulphuric acid as a by-product. The *Victoria County History* of 1906 has no clear explanation of when this began, but it quotes Samuel Dale, writing in 1730, who wrote that there were two Copperas houses there in 1696. So here we have a case of the erosion being in part beneficial, as, although it washed land away, it created pyritic material for use in the Copperas production.

The report from the Royal Commission of 1912 puts Walton and Felixstowe together, and this is only right; they are on the cusp of being part of Essex at the Walton side. At that time, Felixstowe had a seafront of about 5 miles, with a sea wall and over a hundred protective groynes. The author of the report was rather astounded by the state of things here with regard to erosion:

> With the exception of about 850 yards, the whole length of coastline of this district is subject to erosion; why this length should be an exception to the general rule is difficult to explain, but it always presents a full beach and remains immune from all inroads of the sea, although wholly unprotected. Probably the fact that this portion always presents a full beach is a sufficient answer, a full beach being as good as a groyne.

At the time of that report there had been no close study of rates of erosion and land loss, but the author was at pains to stress the danger of high tides and north-westerly winds. He pointed out an advantage of this specific stretch of coast:

> the sea is very shallow for a distance of 3 miles out; and for a stretch of half a mile, the depth of the water is only one and a half fathoms, so that the force of a heavy sea is very much broken long before it reaches the beach.

An Act of 1902 was used to finance work at Felixstowe; this entailed timber groynes and a sea wall. It seems that the groynes used here were particularly sound, as one writer noted: 'As each successive plank is fixed the groyne becomes complete and the beach makes up, nothing but the tops of the piles being visible, with a full level beach, which is the best of all groynes.'

As far as Walton is concerned, only a few years ago, in 2011, a coastal erosion project was announced, with finance of over £1.2 million. More than 16,000 tons of granite has been put in place. The BBC reported locally that residents have been campaigning for defences for twenty-five years, and the promise from the authority is that the area known as Crag Walk will now slow the rate of erosion. All this is part of the Naze Heritage Project.

Arguably the most famous and well-researched phase of the local history here is that of the Roman occupancy. John Fairclough wrote a study of the Roman castle here, a short stretch south of the estuary of the river Deben, nestling by the inlet known as The Dip. There have been several finds here, and a Roman cemetery is now known to archaeologists. Fairclough notes:

> Perhaps Old Felixstowe's church of SS Peter and Paul was sited here later, at the head of a stream of fresh water flowing down the Dip valley into the sea, because the site was already regarded as sacred and attracted significant later burials in this corner of the existing cemetery.

Fairclough quotes the writer Claude Morley, who describes the situation regarding the encroachment of the sea in Saxon times:

> But now all is completely engulfed by the sea, excepting that the foundations are yet visible at neap tides off Repond Bottom [The Dip]

and just opposite the old church with which it was connected by a valley wherein debris of dwellings occur, as I was informed in 1920 by the old sexton there.

As is so common along this coast, history records finds of archaeological and geological interest here, such as the discovery of two skeletons in a cliff fall in 1853 by Professor Henslow.

The population of the two places taken together c. 1900 was 7,000. But that compares amazingly with figures for 1844, which have the population of Walton then as 907 and that of Felixstowe as 502. The expansion of Felixstowe was rapid in the last decades of the nineteenth century, with the importance of it as a port being confirmed by the building of the new dock. The railway arrived in 1877, linked to the modernisation of the port and the dock, but of course, its location made it an ideal holiday resort as well. In 1960, one guide explained, 'It is a grand centre for all kinds of sailing and yachting, being close to Harwich Harbour and other rivers and estuaries.'

Chapter 6

Suffolk's Atlantis: Dunwich

*Perhaps it is as well that the coast has scanty harbourage, for the sea has been
very cruel to Suffolk and has made its coastline a danger to all mariners ...*
Arthur Mee, *Suffolk*

References to Dunwich have been unavoidable in every stage of
writing this account of lost Norfolk and Suffolk, and the reason for
this is not hard to find. The erstwhile town has received detailed
attention from every category of historian, from the social enquiry to the
marine exploration. It has been the subject of books and documentaries, and
has gone from being the subject of a simple 'fallen into the waves' category
to something almost mythological. The reason for this is plain to see: it was a
hugely important place, and it is a rare event in British history for something
of that major scale to be eradicated.

In 1911, the Royal Commission on Coastal Erosion gave some account of
a response by Mr Miles Burne, one of the trustees of the Dunwich Town
Trustees. He was eager to make it clear that something was being done to
hold back the sea in his town, which in the Middle Ages had been one of the
most important settlements in Suffolk. Mr Byrne said that he was interested
in about 5½ miles of coast 'either as owner or as Chairman of the Trustees'.
He told the commissioners that over the previous sixty-eight years, '168
acres, 1 rood and 36 poles' had disappeared, and he added an account of
some measures he himself had taken:

In 1904 I sunk some faggots, butts uppermost, into the shingle, above
ordinary high water mark, to try and prevent the shingle being washed
on to the marshes. In one place three rows were sunk, 180 yards long
and 6 yards apart; in another a single row 100 yards long. The faggots
were placed touching each other.

Did this have any effect, we want to ask. Mr Byrne said that the measures met with some success 'but cannot be considered permanent'. The last word is the crucially important one in the story of Dunwich – surely the most famous and written about town in Britain that has been destroyed by the sea. Somehow, the place seems to have been cursed or fated with being transitory, ephemeral, vulnerable, yet it was once entirely substantial. It was a thriving town with a vibrant array of industries and plenty to be optimistic about in its first phase of growth.

Such is the iconic status of this atmospheric and beautiful place that even the myths and traditions of lost towns have been argued as having substance. One of the most common 'urban legends' of lost villages and towns is that the church bells may be heard by passers-by, from under the water. This kind of topic is ideal for a feature in *Fortean Times*, perhaps, wrapped around with reflection and analysis, but back in the 1950s, the paranormal studies writer Alasdair MacGregor not only gave a profile of Dunwich's ghostly experience, but he also gave names of people whom he interviewed. For instance, we have this:

> When several inhabitants of this neighbourhood claim to have heard these bells, it is customary to make enquiries over a fairly large area … to ascertain whether, by chance, the bells of some known church happened to be ringing at the time.

Tales of Trials

Leaving aside the paranormal, MacGregor also contributed to our documentary record of Dunwich, as he met many locals and asked about evidence of the lost buildings. He met Edwin Clark, who was then the curator of the Dunwich Museum, and Mr Clark was most informative about losses within his lifetime:

> Edwin Clark, a retired farmer there, at the Red House, mentioned to me that the sea now covered the meadows on which he grazed his cows just thirty-five years earlier. Gone with these meadows were the longshore boats and fishermen's sheds he had known. Gone, too, were

the fisher-folk. The scouring south-easterly tides had borne them all away. They are encroaching, he told me, at the rate of 3 to 4 feet a year.

The town lies under the Dunwich Bight. People over the years have brought up their nets and found chunks of masonry; someone brought up a glass decanter, another one lifted out a metal hinge, 2 feet long. It lies under those waves, encrusted with barnacles and limpets, clay and shingle; it lies, with the outlines still visible to divers and detectable by modern technological devices. In a map made by Hamlet Watling in about 1300, with later information added, Rowland Parker in his book on Dunwich shows the outlines of the coast there, past and present. This represents the town in 1400. To the north is the thirteenth-century harbour mouth, which leads to the river and is close to Walberswick to the north. At the north is Hen Hill, with Cock Hill a little south of that. The network of streets clusters around the churches of St Peter's and St John, and arching around from the south to the west are a series of gateways and a town rampart. On the coast, to the extreme south, is the church of St Nicholas.

The history of the town has distinct phases. In the early Middle Ages, it prospered. In the Domesday Book there is a record of 500 tenants, and there were eighty burgesses who were listed for a particular manor, a burgess being an inhabitant who followed an identified trade. Estimates suggest that by about 1200, there was a population of approximately 6,000. In the second phase, marked by the horrors of the floods late in the 1200s and in the first decades of the next century, there was a gradual shrinkage, until the erosion was not only of the cliffs but of everything within the walls. Mark Bailey, in his edition of *The Bailiff's Minute Book* for the early fifteenth century, notes that in 1334, the town account 'records well over 150 properties, varying from *messuages* [a term used to denote a house, outbuildings, garden and land] and tenements, to shops and brewhouses'.

The fourteenth century in Britain (and indeed in all Europe) was horrendous; it must have seemed to people then trying to earn a living and keep their families going that God and Fate were against them, and the struggles covered several generations. The first thirty years brought widespread famine and war; in the late 1340s, the Black Death began its deadly campaign, decimating communities. On top of all this, in Suffolk, the ports had to withstand the sea. The number of boats involved in the herring season, as Mark Bailey notes, 'certainly declined, from an average of 16.9 in the period 1405, to 10.8 in 1425–29'.

In terms of the inundations in the medieval years, it was in the years from 1270–1340 that the worst losses were suffered. In the terrible gales of 1286, 1328 and in the 1330s, there was the most savage and relentless assault. Mark Bailey again presents some useful details: 'Indeed, after 1286–88 the original harbour mouth at Dunwich was periodically blocked by sand and shingle, and then irredeemably in 1328.'

Dives and Digs

Dunwich was a very important port. Recent work by marine archaeologists and social historians has given us a clear idea of what it would have been like at that time, when politics was violent to say the least, and the kings were constantly levying ships in their campaigns of war. A model made at the Dunwich Museum is there now for visitors to study. It shows, for instance, four main thoroughfares, from Middlegate Street to the north, to the Greyfriars central area; to the south there was a leper chapel and the southern main buttress.

In 2008, a major survey began to find and analyse the seabed and the town remains. A sequence of images showing All Saints Church has been complied, showing that building at eight points in time, from the complete church, with a tower and seven main windows, to 1930, when the sea was surrounding the vestiges of the tower; everything else there had gone. In the process of making scans, the archaeological team found seventy-four potential sites for study. The result of the overall mapping showed that the coast of the Saxon town was about 1,000 metres out from the present one.

In the old town, when the worst floods of the thirteenth century hit, there was an urban area of 1.8 square kilometres. There was a central area with a defensive earthwork, and the probable ruins of the churches of St Peter, All Saints and St Nicholas were located, together with the sites of the Chapel of St Katherine and Blackfriars Friary. The first report states that the northern area of the town 'was largely commercial, with wooden structures associated with the port'.

In August 2015, a typical find was described in the news and archaeological reports:

> The medieval town is currently covered by sand, burying all but the tops of the largest ruins ... [and also the] discovery of a previously unknown wreck. ... The wreck is wooden, with copper sheathing on the hull, which dates to post-1750. The wreck is formed of large wooden ribs, with much stone ballast covering the site.

In 2011 also, there was a project headed by Davis Sear and his team for English Heritage. It points out that later development in the Tudor period added another dimension to the decline:

> Additional physical losses occurred in 1560 and 1570 such that by 1602 the town was reduced to a quarter of its original size. ... Further storms in 1740 flattened large areas of the remaining city, so that only All Saints remained open.

Past Troubles

An important element in Dunwich history is its place in the triumvirate of the towns around this estuary that were always competing commercially: Dunwich, Walberswick and Southwold. Daniel Defoe, when passing through, quoted the old rhyme that gives the origin of the dissension:

> *Swoule and Dunwich and Walderswicke,*
> *All go in at one lousie creeke.*

Grenville Collins, writing in 1692, explained this further: 'Dunwich, Walberswick ... and Southwold go all in at one small creek, and divides into three branches. Dunwich on the south branch, Sole [Southwold] on the north and Walberswick in the middle.'

The history of this conflict includes the salient fact that the Dunwich folk appear not to have used any diplomacy and made efforts to work with the people of the other towns rather than against them. There are accounts, for instance, of money being extorted, such as Sir John de Clavering's making of a stockade from which he insisted on tolls being paid by vessels coming through. He was lord of the manor at Blythburgh, so he had to be obeyed. But there was even outside intervention too, when things came to a head, as in 1331 when a commission of inquiry was held when some Dunwich men were accused of setting about a local ship, owned by a woman in Walberswick called Anastasia Butt. The allegation even included a murder charge.

But Dunwich's destiny was sealed. As H. Alker Tripp explained, the situation in the centuries after the main sea incursions brought steady decline:

In 1540, the church of St John Baptist was taken down, and in the same century three chapels and two gates. In the reign of King Charles I, the foundation of the Temple buildings yielded to the irresistible force of the undermining surges, and in 1667 – on a night of terror for the inhabitants – the sea reached the market place.

Now, visitors have to imagine what once was, as Mr Dutt did in 1901: 'Scarcely realise that old Dunwich is so completely gone. It seems rather that I must have mistaken my bearings and arrived at some other seaboard hamlet; and that if only I went a little further north or south, I should hear the songs of sailors on the old quays, the voices of merchants in the market place; and see streets thronged with the cosmopolitan crown of a busy port.'

The latest comments on the place are not cheery either. In 2011, the David Sear report, referred to earlier in this chapter, has this summary of the state of affairs:

The landward sites are currently under threat from a range of pressures, most notably climate driven coastal recession and inundation. This includes the sedimentary sequences associated with the former harbour. … Seaward, coastal recession is driving the accumulation of silt and migration of sandbanks over the site.

My own quest to understand this coast and its compelling tranche of stories involves a response to this former community that has to fall in line with the comments made by writers, from Defoe through to contemporary poets and travel writers. The feelings are an unsteady mix of a rather Romantic view – that all life is temporary and that we are transient – and the more controlled line of thought that the process of land formation will go on relentlessly, as it always has done. Human settlements within that trajectory have to be seen as equal to the experience of the fauna along here too. But of course, that is too hard and uncompromising. The fact we cannot escape is that we *do* have our own 'Atlantis' here on this coast of holidaymakers and fishermen; we have in Dunwich something to compare with the myths and legends of the flood and the epics such as *Gilgamesh*, which has as its central narrative the consequences of a great inundation – something compelling the heroic in mankind to come forward. And yes, looking at the historical experience of the people of the Suffolk coast, there have undoubtedly been heroes there.

A Place of Farewells

I will return yet again, for a third and final time, to Dunwich, in the next chapter, because the place is a magnet for all those writers who need to lift the scene before them into the realms of philosophical reflection or of plain poetic response. For my part, it has imprinted on my own sensibility the kind of feeling that some writers on Romanticism have called 'ordinary extasy', or in the words of C.S. Lewis, it could be labelled an experience summed up by the phrase 'surprised by joy'. Dunwich is that kind of place, and strangely, I was more moved by the fully human response that such visions of past life give us, by the model of the old town in the Dunwich Museum, which, in some inexplicable way, affects the human sense of empathy as acutely as the sea itself, above that encased, literally petrified town.

In the following chapter, I will look at some examples of how Dunwich has inspired two particular writers; but of course, it has been a place that has provided all kinds of material for writers and artists. Perhaps its impact on Rowland Parker, already discussed in my introduction, is one of the clearest examples of a writer being totally dedicated to telling the full story of a place that is, in the popular imagination and in the guidebooks, only vestigial. In short, it haunts more than artists' imaginations: it has come to represent a story of mythic proportions, and adventures into its mysterious depths will continue for a very long time to come.

Chapter 7

The Coast and the Writers' Perspectives

Surely, if the vicar of every parish, the doctor, the school teacher, and district visitors would undertake to preach the necessity of fresh air ... we should soon have a healthier and stronger physique amongst our working classes.

H.M. Appleby, *Letter to* Country Life

The question might be asked, why do some regions of a country attract more attention than others from writers, artists and composers? The question relates to the topic of aesthetics: the notion that some landscapes are immediately attractive whilst others are condemned to be no more than settings for everyday labour and never seem to draw the seekers after beauty or artistic inspiration. Of course, part of the answer to this is the participation of the media; when an influential person occupies a particular place, the crowds may well follow. As we have seen, this was the case with Overstrand. On a larger scale, in the Lake District, William Wordsworth's writings brought the followers looking for the magic he saw there.

In the case of Norfolk and Suffolk, an answer to that same question invites a facile reply, something along the lines of 'Well, all that sky and all the light ...' That same question and answer explains St Ives in Cornwall, for instance, as a focus for painters. But there is much more to the subject than this. My own take on this – and once more, this relates to my quest to relate to this utterly beautiful coastline – is that there are certain combinations of sounds and evocations here that offer something uniquely appealing. These euphonies have brought the sun-seekers and surfers, the crab pool explorers and the beach sports enthusiasts, as much as they have brought the writers. If anyone wants a deeper explanation of this or perhaps a theory, then they might be disappointed. But I can offer a personal angle on the subject. When I first stood on the pebble beach at Southwold, I had come straight from being a spectator at the Maltings, Snape, forever associated with the work of the composer Benjamin Britten, and the wonderful *Sea Interludes* from his opera *Peter Grimes* was still resonating in my mind.

For that moment, the actual sounds of nature – the shingle under my feet – mixed with the haunting beauty of the interludes, with their almost mystical musical account of a mood of nature, and of the eternal presence of the sea, revealed to me a confirmation of the special communion with the natural world that happens in this part of England.

For these reasons, I want to look at the almost magnetic pull this coast has for creative people. I am aware that a full explanation will be impossible, but of one thing I am convinced: that the greed of the waves and the vulnerable earth have been vital elements in this aesthetic appeal through the ages.

The East Anglian coast may have been shifting through time, the sea taking land here and depositing it elsewhere, and that trend has its geological and social interest, with a historian's curiosity in mind. But the towns and villages, and indeed the deserted, isolated spots, have fascinated and intrigued creative writers also. To understand their testimony to the losses to the North Sea, some kind of tribute to the aesthetic nature of this coast is needed, and with that comes the growth of the resorts, because the writers who were born there saw the changes and the writers who travelled there (like Clement Scott in Sidestrand and Overstrand) made it something significant to them and to their individual body of work.

After a look at how and why the tourists came, along with the day-trippers, the focus will shift to the writers of the coast and how for most it has become as 'regional' in sensibility or documentary interest as anything by Hardy or the Brontës. This will be with the awareness that writing becomes 'regional' often by accident: the writer's sensibility is to the fore, and the place where he or she is rooted or is emotionally attached inevitably colours in the context. The writer may not have overtly intended to be 'regional'. In this case, though, it goes without saying that such a landscape is integral to a writer's vision.

Bracing, Like Skegness

The late Victorian and Edwardian years may have been 'naughty', and they may have been decadent, but they were also years in which there were plenty of fun and games, and a prominent part of this was time at the seaside. There were lots of reasons for this, mainly to do with escaping the demands of work and forgetting the boss and deadlines for a while, but one of the most important reasons was to have fresh air.

In a letter to *Country Life* in 1903, a certain H.M. Appleby wrote, talking about 'the poorer classes':

> They seem to have a perfect dread of fresh air getting into their houses. I know of more than one case in which an entire family has died, one by one, of consumption, and the windows and doors of their houses were always kept shut.

Skegness was certainly 'bracing' and invited you to open your lungs and suck in the sea air, and so were Cromer, Hunstanton, Sheringham, Yarmouth and many more down that East Anglian shore.

A significant element in the story of those coastal towns is their status as absolute magnets for holidaymakers and day-trippers. As so often, the railway was the real impetus behind the transformation of the seaside resorts. In 1888, the access to Cromer and its area by rail was much improved: the Eastern and Midlands Railway ran from Peterborough. This linked with the expresses of the Great Northern line, and a new Cromer Beach station was made, so that arrivals were just a short walk to both Cromer and Sheringham. One report, in *The Morning Post*, added:

> It may be mentioned too, that Norwich, Yarmouth, and the Norfolk Broads may be reached without difficulty from Cromer and Sheringham ... there seems every possibility that the country around Cromer, with its woodlands reaching down almost to the shore ... will soon be more widely known among pleasure-seekers.

If we need to understand to what extent the railways played a part in late Victorian life, a glance at the statistics provided by J. Holt Schooling in *The Strand Magazine* in 1896 will help. He wrote:

> This vast number of 911 million passengers conveyed during the year 1894 would, of course, be still greater if the journeys of the 1,184,861

season ticket holders could be included; but, omitting these passengers, I may say that the number of first class passengers in 1894 was about equal to the whole population of Italy.

As with so much development in the nineteenth century, the railways were the impetus behind social change. With the railways came hotels in the string of resorts along the East Anglian coast; the Great Eastern Railway had hotels in Harwich and Hunstanton, for instance, by 1900. As early as 1863, there was a line from London to Wells; this took in Downham Market, Lynn, Burnham Westgate and Burnham Overy, as well as Holkham Staith. There was also a line to Norwich via Cromer, but for the coast at that time, the line from London to Yarmouth opened up the Suffolk resorts, having Kessingland, Blythburgh, Gorleston and Lowestoft on the route. In 1862, the Lynn and Hunstanton Railway, extending only 15 miles, nevertheless covered Lynn, Wolferton, Dersingham, Snettisham, Heacham and Hunstanton.

For Norfolk, the Eastern Counties Railway serviced North Norfolk at this early period, but it was a while after that decade before the resorts on the Norfolk coast were opened up. It was the establishment of the Midland and Great Northern Joint Railway in 1893 that brought the revolution in terms of making the Norfolk coast accessible. As railway historian Nigel Welbourn summarises:

> No fewer than four lines converged on Melton Constable, from Cromer, Norwich, Yarmouth and King's Lynn. The town possessed its own workshops, which made many of the M&GN's locomotives. ... It became known as 'The Crewe of North Norfolk'. The coast run was a section called the North Norfolk Railway, and that extended from Holt to Sheringham, an offshoot from the main line, which went south to Yarmouth Beach.

In more recent times, the rail journeys in that part of the land were, according to one diarist quoted by Nigel Welbourn, interesting but dated:

> 'Monday, 6 April 1964. Today we went only as far as Sheringham. Melton Constable was closed on a Saturday night. We sat in the train at Sheringham until someone came up to ask where we were going.

"Melton Constable closed last week," he said in a Norfolk accent. We were very disappointed.'

Yet the M&GN railway was keen to advertise its holiday route in Norfolk as being 'The Royal Route to Broadland', and it issued a poster showing pictures of Sandringham, Caister Castle, Yarmouth, Gorleston, the cliffs, Mundesley and Hickling Broad. By 1875, the London publishers were catering for the railway travellers to East Anglia, and guidebooks were issued, such as the solid volume from John Murray (Byron's publisher) and, of course, *Bradshaw's Guide*. Murray's was much more detailed on the locations along the routes, and the *Handbook* of 1875 covering Suffolk, for instance, offers a series of specific routes, so that 'Route 16' goes from Ipswich to Yarmouth. It gives essential information such as the name of the hostelry: 'South Lowestoft – Inn; Royal Hotel, a very large, well furnished, commodious house, with moderate charges, pleasantly situated close to the pier, and at the extremity of the esplanade. The Harbour Hotel, near the above, well conducted, with moderate charges.'

The Railway Age had brought with it the opening up of this previously distant, isolated and beautiful region of Britain – now becoming quite the opposite of Clement Scott's Poppy Land. The railways opened up the villages and helped them to become resorts, and with the sun–seekers and railway enthusiasts come the artists and writers.

To recount the history of the losses and gains of beach and cliffs in the seaside towns would demand the extent (and weight) of an encyclopaedia. Every seaside place on this coast has its spin-off histories and biographies, and some of these relate to the lost places, as with the Poppy Land saga. But nevertheless, some of the irresistible narratives are there regarding the special qualities of particular places, so that the seaside locations do not all meld into one generic notion of the same experience. Each had its own identity, and Poppy Land is one special instance of this.

The Writers' Perspectives

Writers and artists played an important part in the opening up and media presence of the resorts, once the railways had arrived, of course. A combination of guidebooks and individual publications contrived to make locations popular. If celebrities stayed there, then the work of the marketing people was done, as in Arthur Conan Doyle's fondness for the golf course at Cromer. But certain works became classics of local writing, such as Ernest Suffling's *The Land of the Broads*, published in 1892. He wrote this explanation of the readership he imagined, and it tells us so much about the attractions of East Anglian resorts and idyllic hinterland: 'Written for the use of all who take an interest in one of the quaintest and most Old-World parts of England, either from an archaeological, historical, picturesque or sporting point of view.'

Suffling was keen to offer practical advice on such things as boating and fishing; he has a very accurate and documentary account of what a duck decoy is, for instance, but when it comes to the seaside experience, he knows that people have bought his book in order to have some guidance in knowing what there is to see, in that age of burgeoning consumerism:

> In the centre of the Parade, facing the sea, stands the Sailors' Home, a large building in the Italian style of architecture. Great as are the resources of this institution, during stormy weather on several occasions, they have been tried to their utmost, nearly every bed being occupied by wrecked sailors and fishermen. The museum, on the first floor, is free, and contains many curious things.

What is of special interest for the present enquiry, though, is the effort of the resorts to settle the problems of erosion and flood – as much as possible, at least – and that has meant expenditure and struggles with financiers as well as with *geomorphology*, the study of land forms and the creation or change of them. This has seen the development of piers, groynes, jetties and sea walls with their promenades.

Suffling was writing creatively as well as in the role of guide and mentor. But he had his poetic side, his lyrical voice, and he was writing at a time when several writers and poets had already made Norfolk or Suffolk parts of their oeuvre. Suffling was there, writing his best-seller, in the midst of the expansion of coastal holidays and the opening up of the seaside vacation to the new crowds of urban commuters. The social history of the 1890s tells us that educational and healthy holidays were being mediated in all kinds of ways, from such popular reads as Jerome K. Jerome's *Three Men in a Boat* to the early series of travel guides such as the *Little Guide* series by Methuen, appearing at the turn of the century, with the Norfolk volume coming out in 1902.

Suffling was of that generation of writers who saw in Norfolk and Suffolk a region of beauty and irresistible fascination; he also wrote adventure books for boys and was an artist. Sadly, he did not have a long life: he died in 1911 at Happisburgh, aged only 55. There is no doubt that his book on the Broads did a great deal to mediate the uniqueness of that often idyllic part of the land, and he was writing about a coast that had already been the home of many writers who were born there.

Every province of Britain has its advocates in art and literature; if we look back through time, tracing the development of writing from the distant corners of the land, the regional poets, novelists and prose writers are there. In the nineteenth century in particular, writers came along whose work may be compared to the best in regional writing, and of course, William Wordsworth being such a massive influence on these genres of work from the regions, he is often there behind the thinking and feeling expressed in the books.

The literature from this coast gives us another interesting angle on the shores, marshes and indeed the lives of people there. If reference keeps only to the nineteenth century, the list is impressive, including George Crabbe, Edward Fitzgerald, H. Rider Haggard and Algernon Swinburne; of course, Clement Scott has to be added, and Arthur Conan Doyle should be included for the origins of his *Hound of the Baskervilles*. In the twentieth century there has been H. Alker Tripp, Lilias Rider Haggard, Graham Swift, Ronald Blythe, W.G. Sebald, Ronald Fletcher, Rowland Parker and Edward Storey.

This chapter looks at some of these writers and their work as it relates to the sea and the shore; reading them gives us especial insights into the experience of living with this landscape, and with the weight of that dynamic and testing social history behind every confrontation with the elements. Interestingly, in addition to this, there have been people who have played the role of host and hearty friend to many writers who came to Suffolk, and the perfect example of this is surely Edward Clodd, who although being born in Margate in 1840, became a Suffolk man, as his family moved to Aldeburgh.

His family history lay in Suffolk and he came to love his home so much that later in life he made Aldeburgh the place where various literary types came to spend some leisure time with him. He was rich enough to have homes in both London and Suffolk, and had wide cultural interests, ranging from folklore to popular science.

Clodd became Suffolk Secretary to the Prehistoric Society of East Anglia, at the time of the Great War; it is consequently easy to see where his interests lay, being close to those cliffs and their treasures for the collector. He also became a leading light in the Omar Khayyam Club, a group who were inspired by the great translated poem *The Rubaiyat of Omar Khayyam*, by Edward Fitzgerald, who was from Boulge in Suffolk.

The list of his writer friends who went to Aldeburgh is very long, and includes Thomas Hardy, George Gissing, Samuel Butler and Holman Hunt. In a chapter from the autobiography of James Milne, we have a first-hand account of a visit to Clodd in which Milne travelled by train from London with Thomas Hardy, and during the stay there, he took a picture of Hardy on Aldeburgh beach with Clodd.

This account comes in a chapter of an obscure work, *The Memoirs of a Bookman*, by James Milne. Milne was at the very hub of mid- to late Victorian literary Britain; his book includes encounters with dozens of writers, and close friendships with a number of these, as well as a cavalcade of minor figures. In his chapter on Suffolk he gives us a profile of Edward Clodd, as well as of Hardy. His book has that photo, showing Hardy and Clodd, smartly dressed in suits, and Hardy with a fedora on his bald head; Clodd looks rather like a railway stationmaster, with a shiny peaked cap and a waistcoat with a fob watch.

The chapter is set at Aldeburgh, and he puts Clodd and his home in the context of that atmospheric place:

Edward Clodd's hospitality was as simple as it was perfect, for while he thought of his guests all the time he let them be at home in their own fashion. Outside, on the October occasion which I have been recalling, the wind was lashing coldly from the North Sea and the night was deepening into darkness. The waves broke on the shingle with the heavy beat which comes from deep water, because Aldeburgh has real salt-tanged ocean, just as it keeps its ancient, long-shore atmosphere of rope and tar.

Milne gives a comfortable, domestic account of the party and the dinner, at which a bunch of literary types enjoy some conviviality. This was in the 1890s, when the world of the arts was one in which clubbable men could be as sociable as they liked, as clubs and societies were being formed on anything from Shakespeare to ballad writing. In Aldeburgh, they chatted of other writers, such as Stevenson and Trollope, but Milne himself was aware that the visitors were out of their comfort zone, and he notes, taking a trip around the bay with Clodd in his yacht, the Lotus: 'Not easy to navigate was the Suffolk Alde with its twisting shoals and its mud banks, where wild birds swarmed and cried.'

The most important literary club for Clodd and friends in Suffolk was their Omar Khayyam Club, because this was one of many that had sprung up across the country, when Edward Fitzgerald's great poetic translation of *The Rubaiyat of Omar Khayyam* was enjoying phenomenal success. Fitzgerald was a Suffolk man, and George Meredith, the novelist, according to Milne, when at a Club meeting, gave an insightful comment: 'Fitz is good Suffolk soil, the most pleasing of Fogies. His literary taste in the classics is quite sound, and infantile out of them.'

Sebald and Swinburne

This is the ideal point at which to look at the ways in which the communities were lost to the sea, and to consider the thrall of the Suffolk and Norfolk coasts that impressed so many writers and poets. In the course of my narrative, I have touched on George Crabbe and Clement Scott, as they gave readers powerful descriptive writing on Southwold, and on Overstrand in particular. The impact of Ernest Suffling has also been noted. But there has been another, much more profound impact of this coast on writers, and in general this ranges from Romanticism, Wordsworthian in manner, to the absorption of the destructive waves and winds into great, overarching metaphors for life and belief.

Before considering the writers Sebald and Swinburne, a glance at H. Alker Tripp will help to pinpoint a certain pattern in the attitudes of these writers. Tripp's main career was as a police administrator; he was born in 1883 and his father was Receiver for the Metropolitan Police District, so that profession was in his blood. Alker himself was to become involved in the workings of the Police Recruiting Board and later he was largely responsible for the planning and formation of the police college, which came into being in the regime of Lord Trenchard.

But he was also a talented artist and writer, and he wrote several books that he illustrated himself, the most relevant here being *Suffolk Sea Borders*, of 1926. His love for the sea and sailing, together with his artistic skills, made this book not only a travel work, but also an impassioned account of the beauties of Suffolk; he builds into his descriptive prose a continuing elegy to the lost Suffolk he sees or is aware of. For instance, he fastens on the obscure community of Goseford – today being 'Gosford'. Even the most standard reference works of earlier times give very little detail of this place, but Tripp places this in the context of the landscape that interests and excites him constantly:

> True enough, we had awakened in the twentieth century and not the thirteenth. The dozen roofs on the low shore could claim no likeness to the port of Ipswich, and greater than Lowestoft or Yarmouth, then places unknown. The coastline was empty and deserted; no traffic, no industry.

Tripp, police administrator and yachtsman, is transformed by Suffolk; the poet in him reaches out for something around him that mixes and confuses a sense of time. When he goes on to work hard to recreate Goseford for the reader, it is with an impulse to bring a past reality alive through lists and specifics:

> Yet Goseford was the very name of which has perished, was wont to contribute its own vessels for the needs of the Crown. When, in 1342, there was a call upon the ports of Suffolk for shipping the expedition of Sir Walter Manny to France, Ipswich sent fourteen vessels, Goseford fifteen, Dunwich four and Orford one.

This attitude is apparent in Fitzgerald and Swinburne; their best work incorporated the lines of thought and feelings drawn from the shore and seascapes of Suffolk. Other artistic media have played with the effects and influences of the sea on the creative mind, of course. One example of visual art that has come close to the themes I am about to explain in the writers is in Maggi Hambling's huge seashell metal creation at Aldeburgh, *Scallop*. Writer Patrick Barkham went to see her and he describes the responses to this and to her statements about the sea, too. He writes:

> Early on, some locals plotted to topple *Scallop* in the night, incensed by its prominence on the beach, and disappointed that its inscription, 'I hear those voices that will not be drowned', a quote from Britten's opera, *Peter Grimes*. ... In spite of the grumbles, the sculpture has survived. I conceived it as somewhere for somebody to sit alone, thinking about life and death and looking at the horizon and all those deep things.

John Betjeman, not known for flights of great metaphorical generalisations, felt the same thing but expressed it more as an artisan than an artist when he said, in a film about Norfolk churches as he stood at Cley church:

> This is Cley-next-the Sea. The sea is now quite a long way off. It is a tiny place but it's got an enormous church. They must have had hopes of it being very much bigger ... and look at the porch – built I should think about 1430. Very delicately done, almost another church in itself ... and slapped on to it very coarsely, a sundial. Time suddenly stuck into eternity.

This is exactly where we have to begin in order to understand the approaches and literary responses to this shore by writers, and I'm taking the examples of Algernon Swinburne and W.G. Sebald to understand what kind of impact the lost land has had on the imagination. Swinburne, writing at the height of the Victorian doubt about the place of God and Divine Nature in the scheme of things, impressed his own melancholy on to the Suffolk coast. Sebald, writing at the opening of the twenty-first century, placed the same coast and the lost communities within a challenging new literary framework, forcing out very modern significance in the losses of such a grand scale as that of Dunwich.

Swinburne's *By the North Sea*

One of the oldest available metaphors for a poet writing of life and death is the sea. The action of waves, the ebb and flow of the water, and the incomprehensible immensity of an ocean all reach out to a poet's need for images to express aspects of the human condition. In the mid-Victorian years in particular, the sea off the east coast of England was used as an integral part of several poets' writing on abstractions such as life, death and belief. In 1867, Matthew Arnold wrote *Dover Beach*, which has constantly been reprinted. It offers one of the great templates of such imagery, perhaps encapsulated in the lines:

> *The sea of faith*
> *Was once, too, at the full, and round earth's shore*
> *Lay like the folds of a great girdle furled.*
> *But now I only hear*
> *Its melancholy, long, withdrawing roar,*
> *Retreating, to the breath*
> *Of the night-wind, down the vast edges drear*
> *And naked shingles of the world.*

Arnold neatly put together the all-embracing sea imagery to express his low state of mind and his profound doubts.

Another classic poem of the age that deals with the sea, faith and death is G.M. Hopkins's *The Wreck of the Deutschland*. This passenger ship had been wrecked in a blizzard 23 miles off Harwich, in 1875. There were five Franciscan nuns on board, and Hopkins, a Jesuit, dedicated the poem to them. Again, he uses the sea imaginatively: '*Thou mastering me / God! Giver of breath and bread / world's strand, sway of the sea.*'

Into this context of the poetic genre of sea and death, enter the poet Algernon Swinburne. Around this same time, with his mind very well read in many branches of literature, Swinburne came to know Suffolk reasonably well. As is the case with so many writers, he could not help but be influenced by the lost places he imagined out under the sea. But even before he came to Suffolk, he had a horrendous encounter with the perilous waves. This was in Cornwall, and his biographer, Philip Henderson, has described what happened, quoting Swinburne's own words:

> I had to run round a point of land which the sea was rising around, or be cut off in a bay to which to my cost I had just found the cliffs impracticable; so without boots or stockings I just ran at it and into the water and up and down over some awfully sharp and shell-encrusted rocks, which cut my feet to fragments, had twice to plunge again into the sea, which was filling all the caves and swinging and swelling heavily between the rocks.

He survived, but only just, coming out 'like a drenched rag' and with multiple deep cuts. This fear must have stayed with him. Years later, he was in Suffolk, and he was to write several poems related to this experience. In a letter to William Rossetti from Southwold, he writes of a place that was obviously the trigger to some kind of revelation to him as a poet:

> I have found a place that would have delighted Shelley – a lake of fresh water only parted from the sea by a steep and thick pebble-ridge through which a broad channel has been cut in the middle a little above the lake, to let off the water in a flood-time. … It is so unutterably lonely that I thought instantly how like this beautiful wood must be in winter to Dante's wood of suicides.

Here, referring to the great classic poem by Dante, *The Divine Comedy*, which imagines heaven, purgatory and hell, Swinburne projects his feelings and his literary ideas on to the Suffolk location. We can imagine just how much more the thought of Dunwich affected him, after that one very specific inspiration from a seaside lake. The work he wrote that brings out the thought of Dunwich is *By the North Sea*. In one stanza he reflects on the lost community very directly:

As the souls of the dead men disburdened
And clean of the sins that they sinned,
With a lovelier than man's life guerdoned
And delight as a wave's in the wind,
And delight as the wind's in the billow,
Birds pass, and deride with their glee
The flesh that has dust for its pillow
As wrecks have the sea.

He builds up through the poem the sense of a defined time, within the span of eternity, until his final image of '*And sweeter than all that we call so/the seal of their slumber shall be/till the graves that embosom them also/be sapped of the sea.*'

It can be seen in Swinburne's poetry just how the Victorians made use of the 'German Ocean', as they knew it, as an image that enabled them to tackle questions of loss and time in an age in which Christian belief had been shaken by Charles Darwin's *The Origin of Species* of 1859. To the artists and thinkers of that age of doubt, places such as Dunwich offered a powerful metaphor, a symbol of how the greatest human communities could be swept away – as Atlantis had supposedly been in the days of antiquity, which these writers would all have been familiar with in their grammar school or public school education.

In Swinburne's case, his experiences in Suffolk made a deep mark on his emotions. His biographers tend to agree that at the time of his discovery of that lake and the shingle ridge, he was in a very depressed mood (of course, he mentions suicide as a theme) and much of that is imprinted on the poem.

In complete contrast we have the section on Dunwich in W.G. Sebald's innovative prose work *The Rings of Saturn*, published in 2002, a year after his death. Sebald's books are challenging mixes of subjects and reflections. In this book he has a narrative spine placed in East Anglia, but the topics within chapters range from Nazi atrocities to Joseph Conrad and from the Taiping Rebellion to the story of Roger Casement (hanged for espionage during the Great War). But there are themes here, and in his reflections on the end of Dunwich he includes one of his most successful passages concerning the merciless process of history, and how human communities exist and move helplessly with what historians might call the metanarrative – the large, overarching story above and beyond the ordinary person.

With this in mind, Sebald does what anyone seeing Dunwich would try to do: imagine the end. As we imagine what lies beneath the sea there, and as we think of what it must have been like to live there and experience the great flood of the thirteenth century, so Sebald takes up that challenge and attempts to account, as in this extract:

> All we know for certain is that they [the defences] proved inadequate on New Year's Eve, 1285, a storm tide devastated the lower town and the portside so terribly that for months afterwards no one could tell where land ended and the sea began. There were fallen walls, debris, ruins, broken timbers, shattered ships' hulls, and sodden masses of loam, pebbles, sand and water everywhere. And then on 14 January 1328, after only a few decades of rebuilding ... an even more fearful disaster occurred.

The nearest point of reference we have to this is possibly the great floods of 1953. At the end of January that year, a great surge was linked to an abnormally high tide. The result was that, by the end of the floods, 307 people were dead and 40,000 were homeless. One witness from Felixstowe said to the press, 'I don't know how long we were up on the roof but the next thing I knew there was a policeman by my side.'

The photographic record of the disaster says more than words can do: a street in Great Yarmouth, where a man, wellington-booted, walks knee-deep in water while a woman from an upstairs window calls for help; a street corner scene in which women are serving out hot soup from a bin; in Heacham, Norfolk, five women root around in a smashed houseboat, looking for their possessions; and at Salthouse, a basic flood warning siren is installed and tested.

Something like that massive level of fear and alarm must surely have been the case in Dunwich, back in the days when the people's rulers were distant and more concerned with war and wealth than protecting their coasts. Many in 1953 started asking where the experts had been, the ones who should have known this flood was possible. Could it have been prevented? Experts responded of course, and one provided the ultimate fact that would unsettle the population, from Felixstowe to Blakeney: the east coast is sinking by 150 mm. Every 100 years.

The writers such as Swinburne and Sebald, and before them George Crabbe and Clement Scott, were concerned with making this coast a place where the reality of land tumbling – or already tumbled – into the North Sea, either a place for idyll or for contemplation. In both cases, it has to be said that the tendency has been to be more involved in the thoughts and feelings urged by the brooding immensity of the sea off East Anglia than the minutiae of daily life. But the documentary comment has been there too – in paintings and drawings perhaps, most often. Regarding the written testimony, there is no doubt that the lost land and the submerged material of past communities have maintained the limelight as far as literature goes.

From both Swinburne and Sebald, in very different ways, of course, the importance of the Norfolk and Suffolk that once were, and are now no more, is a powerful and significant element in their work. For the rest of us, their writing makes it clear that while the artefacts such as bones, tools and pots are informative, there is something entrancing and compelling about the literary record provided by the poets.

During my research for this book, an Ipswich man said to me, ''Course, you know that the Rubaiyat chap was from just up the coast … odd fellow he was!'I soon discovered the charming eccentricity of Edward Fitzgerald, and his love of this restless coast, and the more I thought about his life, the more I came to see that he was drawn to the opposite of creativity, as well as to making stories and compiling poems: he was, in fact, fascinated by what was always slipping away. The Viennese of the last century, when the Hapsburg Empire existed, had a word for that sense of slippage, the ebbing away of human communities, the dissolution of anything that seemed solid and dependable. They called it *Das Gleitende*, and the adjective going with it is *glatt* – slippy. Somehow, that strongly Germanic word suits the violence and destruction of the waves of what was, after all, once known as the German Ocean.

It comes as no surprise then, to learn that so much of the writing about this coast has been concerned with what has slipped away – and that means more than the cliffs.

Chapter 8

Some Conclusions

The design of our defences was based around timber revetments, but these collapsed and haven't been replaced.
                    Clive Stockton, North Norfolk District Council

The range of subjects related to coastal erosion and the sea's destruction of communities has meant excursions into geological concepts of time, elegiac contemplation of the sea and the lost land, and of course, it has meant that attempts have had to be made to envisage past human gatherings, from the Stone Age to the very recent. What strikes anyone trying to take in the sheer variety of sea and land interplay along Norfolk and Suffolk is the shifts from such land as the North Alluvial Plain, seen typically at Cley, down to the marshes and shingle banks of Suffolk. It comes as no surprise to learn that this coast attracts every kind of naturalist and geologist.

Exploring and researching this area has meant that I, a mere landlubber from the industrial North, have had to look far more closely at rocks, earth, river and sea than I ever did previously. The result of that enquiry is that I have begun to understand how people have coped over the centuries with the certainty that nature cannot be tamed and controlled. Perhaps most significantly in this respect was the discovery that, in many places – as recorded in Maggs's diary, for instance – fishermen's dwelling places were down close to the sea. It has not all been a story of soft cliffs and powerful tides.

Something in me does not want to end this book with talk of surveys, marine exploration, or future plans by rural district councils. No, I feel that I have had a quest, as in my title, and that the quest has really been about what this coast and the thought of its ragged history can do for the writer. To say that it is a salubrious, sobering experience is an understatement. It is much more than that. By some almost magical process, the sea and shore here changes anyone who engages with it for aesthetic or for romantic reasons. (I wrote the last sentence with a small 'r' on purpose, to escape the cliché of that Wordsworthian contemplation of nature that tends to limit enquiry as well as explanation.

No, I want to conclude with reflections that open out into free exploration in the mind, just as the feet have done, walking some of these wonderful places.

Early in my planning of this book, I was looking for the bigger story behind the local one. This is something I always do in order to place my narrative, set it in a framework, so to speak. I found it after some thought about flooding generally over the last fifty years, within my own lifetime. This was in the establishment of the Thames Barrier, which was up and running in 1982, and Tony Aldous wrote about it in *The Illustrated London News*.

He wrote about the threat to London by 'freak tides' and referred to a medieval event that shook me; I was astonished by the thought of it:

> In 1236, a medieval eyewitness reported a flood in which 'in the great Palace of Westminster men did row with wherries in the midst of the hall.' ... The risk of a tidal surge overtopping the river walls – in 1970 put at one in ten – results from a combination of England's south-eastward tilt, the fact that London is sinking on its clay bed, and the risk of a very high tide coinciding with a depression entering the North Sea and strong north winds.

That last sentence is truly staggering. I had never had any idea that England had a 'south-eastward tilt' nor that London was sinking. But these alarmist thoughts, and the sheer wonder of the Thames Barrier as an engineering achievement, spurred me on to try to include some kind of wider enquiry into my stories of East Anglia. Of course, I had to keep this a slim element in the book, as this is a light read for the general reader, not for the scientist. I hope I succeeded in giving some kind of acceptable framework to the East Anglian coast story.

In 2013, a huge area of seabed off the East Anglian coast was dredged by the Crown estate. The reason for this is that the marine aggregate and sand taken could be used for building materials. The report on this pointed out, 'Marine aggregate is also commonly used to support beach nourishment schemes, providing benefits to communities, local economies and the environment.' Almost 4 million tons of sand and gravel were taken from the coastal beds off Happisburgh, Southwold, Clacton and Southend.

In the course of that report, which comfortingly assures the reader that no holes were made in the seabed, and that dredging plays no part in worsening the situation regarding the erosion, it was pointed out that, as shown by Chris and Sarah Weston in 1994, since the fourteenth century, the loss of land between Cromer in the north and Dunwich in the south had ranged from 15 kilometres at Cromer and Dunwich to perhaps 2 kilometres off Newton Cross, south of Yarmouth. This is all simply a statement of a factual record, but there is also the factor of the offshore banks, which gather off Yarmouth while the sea continues to erode the cliffs at the land side of these great sand collections. But it is not all bad news, because from Southwold to Orford, we are told that 'relict river sediments are now dredged: no feed to inshore banks or coastline'. In other words, as has happened through the centuries, some areas are protected and others are left to their fate.

This has been the pattern in history – cycles of protective work done and then abandonment. The sandbanks are buffers to wave action, but not at the coast itself, which is not affected. The future for the Sandlands coast therefore seems to be, as in Yorkshire, for instance, that investment decisions are and have always been made, alongside any other random projects relating to industrial or scientific study or produce.

The people and communities that have lived with such erosion and loss of land over the centuries have emerged as being much more interesting than the physical geography. A social geography always exists alongside the actual details of the land. In searching for some way of explaining the firm resilience of the Norfolk and Suffolk people living on these coasts I needed some kind of expression of their learning and their wisdom gained from harsh experience, such as we may see in photos like the one in Cromer Museum showing eight fishermen in their ganseys and working trousers, lined up by baskets and boards. The man who put this line of thought most powerfully has to be novelist and ship's master Joseph Conrad, who wrote, in his first novel, *An Outcast of the Islands*:

The old sea; the sea of many years ago, whose servants were devoted slaves and went from youth to age or to a sudden grave without needing to open the book of life, because they could look at eternity reflected on the element that gave the life and dealt the death.

Most striking of all aspects of the subject is – and this is something that must open out the material history into the imaginative dimension – that this coast, from the sands and shingles of The Wash and the Glaven Ports down to the long creeks and floods of Suffolk, inspires every kind of artist and creative mind. I have found it impossible to study these shores and cliffs without moving reflection from the merely descriptive to the impassioned and lyrical figurative language available. That is, for reasons previously explored, this coast makes it impossible for the mind to dwell on the everyday, the prosaic and the rational. Something about the vista of level sea contrasted with its dynamic and destructive moods compels one to consider its identity as a thing of moods. The fact that earlier writers tended to write about the North Sea as if it were a creature – using the literary ploy known as the *pathetic fallacy* – tends to influence the modern witness, every time the latest press report and alarming pictures of disintegrating cliffs makes the news.

Avoiding any such emotional response to the lost places is a tough demand, though; in the 1930s, Arthur Mee put the case for a plea for our empathy towards all that abandoned society when he wrote:

Certain it is that lands and villages and the graves of men, who are so near kin to us that they seem to belong to yesterday, lie buried here beneath the salt billows of the North Sea, their place and habitation blotted out, but their story known to us through the ancient records of their town.

I had initially ventured into Norfolk expecting no real surprises, as I had been several times before, but when you go with a writer's mind into a field of enquiry, somehow a magical process starts to happen, and your mind begins to form stories from everyday objects. The Norfolk and Suffolk beaches have a supply of such things, which is why beachcombing there is such a joy. In my case, as I had studied and written about the Yorkshire coast not long before my visits into East Anglia, I expected much more of the same. Yet no, other than the fact that cliffs sometime crumble like sandcastles kicked over by children, there were no substantial differences. I recall saying to myself, walking in a strong wind and looking out at Blakeney, *Never such skies ... and never such confusion of sky and spray.*

Finally, the other principal reflection after these accounts of sea against land is that compared with my native Yorkshire, this coast is one, in many places, in which the river courses, mud flats and marshes have eaten in from the coast to make such a string of fascinating places as the Burnhams. Here, I have walked from The Hero inn all the way up to Hunstanton and felt like dwelling at almost every turn and every sight of water. The reason for this, I see now that I have returned and I sit in my office, is that I was, essentially, in a past location, and time as we think of it in the twenty-first century had been swatted so that it stopped buzzing. Again, I thought, as I emerged into Old Hunstanton, never such carelessness about the clock and the watch. Norfolk had freed me from such slavery.

Being in a place such as the Burnhams reminds one of the fact that, in Norfolk, the sea is always there, regardless of where you are: it has penetrated so much and so far. Peter Flatman has put this well. I asked him about his awareness of the sea when he grew up in Diss in the 1950s, and his answer was:

> I was aware of the terrible floods of 1953 but apart from the Waveney being swollen I was not aware of any dramatic happenings in Diss or Bressingham, and yet it always amazed me when in school assembly we sang the song with this refrain: *For those in peril on the seas ...* It seemed to my young mind unimportant because we were dozens of miles from the sea.

Yet, if he had looked at history, which of course he has done since, he would have been reminded that the long invasive rivers brought the sea to many a doorstep.

One image lingers, and it is not even an image from the land facing the sea. This is St Clement's church at Burnham Overy. I learned that part of it was once a village school. So, I remember thinking, the ghosts of the children are there, still reciting arithmetic tables; all gone, like the villages and hamlets I have chronicled. The sea is not the only destroyer of peace and stability. Yet in fact, the sea is the very embodiment of that relentless force of change that has plagued poets since records began, and it explains why Shakespeare chose to use the waves as images in his great sonnets, as in these lines from *Sonnet 60*:

> *Like as the waves make towards the pebbled shore,*
> *So do our minutes hasten to their end;*
> *Each changing place with that which went before,*
> *In sequent toil all forwards do contend.*

The poetry exists alongside the more prosaic, and four centuries ago, Robert Reyce, writing more on the bases of wealth in Suffolk, made this comment on the bedrock of the county:

> Neither is here to be found any quarries of stone for the use of building, our best stone is that smooth pebble which serveth us for paving of courts and streets, and is either gathered in the plowed [*sic*] fields, or fetched from the brooks and rivers, where through the extremity of the current it is washed out of the banks or else brought from the sea shores, where at every tide it is washed and driven up through the violence of the waves and surges of the sea beating up the same.

It is hard to think of a better, more expressive account of that natural, organic relationship of man to physical environment; the evidence of what Reyce is explaining is everywhere in Norfolk too, with the thousands of homes dotted with flint in squares by the side of the red brick or stone. Somehow – and this is hard to explain – in Norfolk and Suffolk, there is always the sense for the traveller that all life there has been lived with an ear to the earth, listening, sensing, being integral to every inch of the home landscape. This helps to explain why writers and artists become embedded in the place, against the trend of nature here, which is often come and gone in a blink. That coast will keep shifting and shuffling, being mutable and malleable to the sea. Perhaps the people of Happisburgh have the most constructive approach – to move out of the way and let the sea loose. Its hunger cannot be abated, merely delayed.

After previously writing about the Yorkshire coast in my companion volume in this series, it has been inevitable that I would compare and contrast. That comparison has made it plain that East Anglia presents more landscape variety, and stretches of its coast tend to absorb water, in a process of deposition; but that also means that when the sea does destroy land, as at Bacton or Happisburgh, for instance, in very dramatic ways, the sight of such geomorphological change is so apparent. Beneath all the turmoil of nature's determination to take land and steal people's precious land here, history has shown that repeatedly, local families have adapted and restructured their lifestyles and objectives. The two coastlines have presented me with stunning contrasts, and looking at the very different social histories of the people there has offered new angles on social history.

In spite of all the elements described in the above tales of that battle between sea and land, the decisive thought I am left with concerns something almost indefinable: that unique quality that brings visitors in their droves in order to experience one of Britain's very best locations for the national pastime of sea-watching.

If we have to locate a place that typifies the contemporary approach to the preservation of the coastline, perhaps the case of Caister-on-Sea in Norfolk is a useful example to end with. Its beauty has attracted several artists recently, perhaps most evocatively Damien Ward, whose painting captures beautifully the zigzag of the lines of groynes, along with the wind-blown sands to the sides of the installation, and the distant wind farm out to sea.

This capture of Caister's compelling beauty, placed by the side of official attitudes to the area expressed by the Policy Unit at North Norfolk, defines the heart of the issue now being mooted by all parties involved in preservation. The official report includes these words:

The long-term plan for the frontage would therefore be to enable the beach and backshore to evolve more naturally by improving the alignment between California and Caister Ness, and allowing the shoreline position to retreat back to a more natural position.

On the surface this looks like defeat, but as the case of Happisburgh confirms, there is much sense in the attitude that allows nature to do its work and then to accentuate the positive by protecting what is most easily worked on.

Clearly, current measures at Caister entail the use of these rather startlingly innovative groynes that have attracted the artists and photographers. The encouraging trend here is that some scientific approaches have designed and constructed something different – a new design that perhaps reduces the tendency of groynes to cause the accumulation of sand where it is not wanted.

As I sat down to write these conclusions, a feature on the evening news reported on the fears in North Lincolnshire and Holderness that the Environment Agency is not doing enough to protect agricultural areas there from a tidal surge such as the devastating one of December 2013. Great stretches of East Anglian coast present a similar concern from residents. But the official short-term policy in Norfolk is in line with the Humber Estuary attitude: 'Only when such adequate mitigating social measures are identified to limit the impact on the lives of individuals and the community, would the long-term change to a managed realignment policy option be implemented.' This is so familiar to students of social history: the formal vocabulary used in the explanation of the official position offers little comfort (and perhaps even less understanding) to residents in areas such as Caister.

In places such as South Ferriby, on the North Lincolnshire coast, reassurance from the Environment Agency always relates matters to expenditure on defences, and of course, there is a consequent prioritizing when it comes to spending the budget available. The officials have to find ways of explaining policy by avoiding a direct statement that heavily populated areas will take precedence in the planning of expenditure.

In my previous volume in this series, the situation on the east coast of Yorkshire is similar to that of Norfolk, but along the Humber, obviously more densely populated places such as Selby, Hessle and Hull will be high on the league table in the accountants' plans. As has so often been the case, villages, hamlets and holiday settlements will be at the back of the queue.

Acknowledgements

Thanks must go first to the *doyen* of East Anglian history, Neil R. Storey, whose books have been invaluable. As usual in my work for writings on social history, conversations with railway and social historian Bryan Longbone have been extremely helpful. Staff at the Brynmor Jones Library, University of Hull, helped in locating some very obscure sources. For the more imaginative dimension, thanks go to the various folklorists who have written on such elusive topics as 'the bells beneath the waves' and other equally enthralling oral tales. For the same reason, thanks to Peter Flatman for his contribution too.

I had many conversations with local people in the course of researching the book, and I would like to give special thanks to Roy, stationmaster at the Weybourne railway station and sheds, and to the fishermen of the coast, who explained the situation for people living and working there today.

For material on Dunwich, special thanks go to Jane Hamilton of the Dunwich Museum, who kindly supplied the image of the museum's model of Dunwich as it was before the inundation. Also, as every writer on the Suffolk coast must agree, the shadow of Rowland Parker presides over every word. Jane's help typified the general attitude I found in conversations with local people: always obliging and welcoming. The result was that I surely learned more about this coast from chats and questions in streets than I did from old tomes in libraries.

Finally, thanks go again to Linne Matthews, my editor, for the usual hard work and assistance.

Bibliography and Sources

Note: Dates of first publication are given in brackets.

Books cited in the text

Anon, *Handbook for Essex, Suffolk, Norfolk and Cambridgeshire*, John Murray, 1875.

A Lynn Sexagenarian, *Personal Recollections*, Thew & Son, 1891.

Arguile, Roger, *Wells-next-the-Sea*, Poppyland Publishing, 2013.

Armstrong, M.J., *An Essay on the Contour of the Coast of Norfolk*, Crouse & Stevenson, 1791.

Barkham, Patrick, *Coastlines: The Story of our Shore*, Granta, 2015.

Bede, *A History of the English Church and People* (completed in AD 731), Penguin, 1970.

Belloc, Hilaire, *Hills and the Sea*, Methuen, 1906.

Betjeman, Sir John, *Coming Home: An Anthology of Prose*, Methuen, 1997.

Blomefield, Francis, *An Essay Towards a Topographical History of the County of Norfolk*, W. Miller, 1809.

Blythe, Ronald, *Akenfield* (1969), Penguin, 1975.

Bottomley, A.F., *The Southwold Diary of James Maggs 1818–1876*, Suffolk Record Society, 1984.

Brooks, Peter, *Cley: Living with memories of Greatness*, Poppyland Publishing, 1984.

Brooks, Peter, *Sheringham: The Story of a Town*, Poppyland Publishing, 1980.

Browne, Sir Thomas, *Urn Burial* (1658), Penguin, 2005.

Crabbe, George, *Tales 1812 and Other Selected Poems* (1812), edited by Howard Mills, Cambridge University Press, 1967.

Crane, Nicholas, *Coast: Our Island Story*, Random House, 2010.

Crane, Nicholas, *Great British Journeys*, Weidenfeld & Nicolson, 2007.

Defoe, Daniel, *A Tour Through the Whole Island of Great Britain* (1724–26), Penguin, 1971.

Dutt, W.A., *Norfolk*, Batsford, 1902.

Ellis, Clarence, *The Pebbles on the Beach*, Faber, 1954.

Evans, George Ewart, *Where Beards Wag All*, Faber & Faber, 1970.

Ferguson-Lees, James & Campbell, Bruce, *Coasts and Estuaries*, Hodder & Stoughton, 1979.

Fitzgerald, Edward, *The Rubaiyat of Omar Khayyam*.

Fletcher, Ronald, *In a Country Churchyard* (1978), Granada, 1980.

Glyde, John, *The Moral and Religious Condition of Ipswich in the Middle of the Nineteenth Century* (1850), SR Publishers, 1971.

Griffiths, Dr Derek, *A History of the Church Building*, Cromer Parish Church, 2016.

Haggard, Lilias Rider, *I Walked by Night*, Oxford University Press, 1982.

Haggard, Lilias Rider, *A Norfolk Notebook*, Faber & Faber.

Harper-Bill, Christopher et alia, *East Anglia's History*, Boydell Press, 2002.

Hedges, A.A.C., *Yarmouth is an Ancient Town*, Jarrold, 1959.

Hedges, Mark (Ed), *Letters to the Editor*, Simon & Schuster, 2012.

Henderson, Philip, *Swinburne: The Portrait of a Poet*, Routledge & Kegan Paul, 1974.

Hewitt, W., *An Essay on the Encroachments of the German ocean along the Norfolk Coast*, Matchett, Stevenson & Matchett, 1844.

Howat, Polly, *Tales of Old Norfolk*, Countryside Books, 1991.

Huchon, Rene, *George Crabbe and his Times*, Frank Cass, 1968.

Laslett, Peter, *The World We Have Lost – Further Explored*, Routledge, 2000.

Long, David, *Lost Britain*, Michael O'Mara, 2015.

Macfarlane, Robert, *The Wild Places*, Granta, 2007.

MacGregor, Alastair Alpin, *The Ghost Book*, Robert Hale, 1955.

Martin, Robert Bernard, *With Friends Possessed: a life of Edward FitzGerald*, Faber & Faber, 1985.

Mee, Arthur, *The King's England: Norfolk: Green Pastures and still waters*, Hodder & Stoughton.

Milne, James, *The Memoirs of a Bookman*, John Murray, 1934.

Milne, Thomas, *A Topographical Map of the County of Norfolk*, the author, 1797.

Monsarrat, Ann, *An Uneasy Victorian*, Cassell, 1980.

Morton, H.V., *In Search of England* (1927), Penguin, 1960.

Nicol, Cheryl, *Sir Berney Brograve: A Very Anxious Man*, Createspace, 2016.

Pryor, Francis, *The Making of the British Landscape*, Penguin, 2011.

Reports of the Late John Smeaton F.R.S, Vol. III, M. Taylor, 1837.

Reyce, Robert, *Suffolk in the XVII Century* (1618), John Murray, 1902.

Scobell, Henry, *An Ordinance for Reviving and Continuing an Act of Parliament for recovery and preservation of many thousand acres of ground In Norfolk and Suffolk surrounded by the Rage of the Sea*, du-Gard & Hills, 1654.

Scott, Clement, *Poppy Land: Papers Descriptive of Scenery on the East Coast*, Carson & Cummerford, 1886.

Sebald, W.G., *The Rings of Saturn*, Vintage, 2002.

Storey, Neil R., *The Lost Coast of Norfolk*, History Press, 2006.

Suffling, Ernest R., *The Land of the Broads*, Benjamin Perry, 1892.

Swift, Graham, *Waterland*, Heinemann, 1983.

Swinburne, Algernon, *Poems and Ballads and Atalanta in Calydon*, edited by Kenneth Haynes, Penguin, 2000.

Swinburne, Algernon, *Swinburne's Collected Poetical Works Vol. II*, Heinemann, 1927.

Taylor, Tim, *The Time Team Guide to the History of Britain* (4 books, no date).

Tuchman, Barbara, *A Distant Mirror: The Calamitous Fourteenth Century*, Ballantine Books, 1978.

Warren, W.L., *Henry II*, Eyre Methuen, 1973.

Welbourn, Nigel, *Lost Lines: Eastern*, Ian Allan, 1995.

Whittow, John, *Geology and Scenery in Britain*, Chapman & Hall, 1992.

Williamson, Tom, *Sandlands: the Suffolk coast and heaths*, Windgather Press, 2005.

Wright, William Aldis (ed), *More Letters of Edward FitzGerald*, Macmillan, 1901.

Official Publications
Anon, *An Ordinance for reviving and continuing an Act of Parliament for the recovery of many thousands of acres in Norfolk and Suffolk*, du-Gard & Hills, 1654.

The Crown Estate: *Aggregate Dredging and the Norfolk Coastline*, Crown Estate, 2014.

Reference works
Anon, *The County of Suffolk: Official Guide*, British Publishing Company, no date.

Anon, *Victorian Travellers' Guide to 19th Century England and Wales* (1864), Bracken Books, 1985.

Castleden, Rodney, *Inventions that Changed the World*, Futura, 2007.

Green, Charles, *The History, Antiquities and Geology of Bacton in Norfolk*, Josiah Fletcher, 1842.

Richardson, John, *The Local Historian's Encyclopaedia*, Historical Publications, 1974.

Robertson, David, *et alia*, *Norfolk Archaeological Unit, Norfolk Rapid Coastal Zone Archaeological Survey*, Norfolk Archaeological Unit, April 2006.

Articles in newspapers and journals/ contributions to books
Anon, 'Britain Can Fight for Her Beaches', *The Observer*, 11 June 1944, p.7.

Anon, 'Disastrous gale', *The Illustrated London News*, 25 October 1862, p.431.

Anon, 'Grand by Name, Grand by Nature and 250 Years Old', *Lincolnshire Life*, October 2016, pp.100–101.

Barringer, J.C., introduction to *Faden's Map of Norfolk*, Larks Press, 2009.

Champion, Matthew, 'Medieval Voices: Recording England's Early Church Graffiti', *Current Archaeology*, June 2016, pp.28–33.

Fussell, G.E., 'A Suffolk Boyhood in the 1820s', *The Suffolk Review*, Vol. 1, No. 4, April 1957, pp. 84–7.

Gibb, Frances, 'A Home at stake in between birds and fossils', *The Times*, 6 December 2008, p.47.

Milligan, Charles, 'The Thames Barrier is Ready', *The Illustrated London News*, Vol. 270, No. 7012, November 1982, pp. 45–9.

Riggs, Christina, 'Murk and Mysteries', *Times Literary Supplement*, 27 May 2016, p.18.

Savage, Michael, 'The Norfolk Village Being Swallowed by the Sea', *The Independent*, 17 August 2008.

Schooling, J. Holt, 'Railway Facts in Fancy Frames', *The Strand Magazine*, Vol. XI, 1896, pp. 641–8.

Thompson, Mark, 'The Brightest and the Best', *Norfolk Coast Guardian*, 2016, p.4.

Society Publications

Forties Gazette, September 2015.

Forties Gazette, September 2016.

M&GN Circle Bulletin, Issue 382, January 1993.

National Piers Society, *Bulletin*, 2016.

Official reports

HMSO Royal Commission on Coast Erosion and Afforestation, Wyman & Sons, 1911.

Internet Sources

www.edp24.co.uk, 'The Haunting Tale of a Waxham Man', Rown Mantell, Eastern Daily Press. This also refers to the author of the biography of Sir Berney Brograve, Cheryl Nicol (see above for details).

'Million-year-old Norfolk Footprints', Steve Connor, see www.independent.co.uk, 7 February 2014.

Norfolk Heritage Explorer: this is a very useful collection of materials and reports relating to county archaeology. The site is www.heritage.norfolk.gov.uk.

'Felixstowe Roman Port', by John Fairclough, see: www.suffolkinstitute.pdfsrv. co.uk.

www.griffmaster-walks.blogspot.

The Times Digital Archive:

'The Clifftop Crusader wins his fight to repel the sea', 21.9.2016.

'Walton-on-the Naze Coastal Erosion Project Completed', see www.bbc.co.uk/news/uk-england-essex, 8 April 2011.

Index